Testimonials from successful interview candidates

"*Case Interviews For Beginners* gave me the confidence I needed to get started with case prep. By walking me through an example case it demystified the whole thing, and allowed me to work out for myself how I should best prepare."

"I knew I needed to get good at cases, I just didn't know where to start. This book was a great introduction."

"There's so much mystique around cases, this book did a great job of making them understandable."

"I wish I'd read this before I dived into case practice – I came to it quite late in the process and found that it answered a lot of questions I didn't even know to ask."

"As a liberal arts major, I was very concerned about my ability to get through a case interview, which I'd heard was designed for MBAs. The book gave me the confidence to be myself and enjoy the interview, and I think that was the key to my success."

"A case interview is like a dance. If you haven't been taught the steps, you'll never succeed."

CASE INTERVIEWS FOR BEGINNERS

By Stephen Pidgeon

Acknowledgements

No book is the work of only one person, and I'd like to thank everyone whose input and encouragement made this possible.

For the many interviews that guided the book as it took shape, I'd like to thank everyone who agreed to give their valuable time and insights.

For editing, special thanks to Ron, Penny and Danielle.

Thanks to Jonathan, Gina, Steve, Paul and everyone at Tuck for supporting my writing endeavors and helping spread the word to a wide audience, and thanks to my many colleagues in career offices around the world for your input and help – I hope this book will be as useful to you and your students as the last one.

Thanks to my friends and colleagues at McKinsey for teaching me so much not only about the content of this book but also about how to follow my energy. I loved working with you and I love vicariously sharing your adventures.

Thanks to Caroline for sharing your writing experiences and making me feel like a writer myself, to Kevin for accompanying me on so many amazing writing journeys, to Lauren for your feedback, and to Wai Kwen for, among many other pieces of useful advice, suggesting that I need an acknowledgements page!

Contents

Introduction 1

    What this book will cover: 1

    Navigating through this book: 2

    Why do I feel qualified to teach you about cases? 3

    What do the experts say? 4

What is a case interview? 5

    What do Sherlock Holmes and Bain & Company have in common? 6

    Not a test of your knowledge, but of your problem solving abilities.......8

Why do interviewers use case interviews? 11

Types of case interview 16

    Brainteaser/market sizing...16

    Classic case...16

    Blue Sky case...17

    Group case 19

Sample cases 20

    Example of a classic case 20

    Analysis of the sample classic case 33

    Example of a market sizing case 44

    Analysis of the sample market sizing case 48

Case interviews test a combination of skills 51

Structure 55

What does unstructured thinking look like?...........................55

Why is structure useful when approaching a difficult problem?...........60

Why is structured thinking useful in the interview?...........................62

How to create a good structure...........................62

How to ensure your structure is tailored to the question 83

Practice drills...........................86

Numerical Analysis...........................88

A reminder of what they are looking for 90

An overview of some useful steps to get through most math issues 94

Setting up a multi-step calculation 100

The mystery of the missing data...........................102

Reading Charts 103

Quality of Thinking 106

Business sense 106

Judgment 111

Creativity...........................113

Game Plan 116

Guiding principles for case prep 118

Last minute prep for when the interview is tomorrow 122

FAQs 124

About the Author...........................131

Introduction

I'm assuming you're looking at this book because you have found out that you will have a case interview at some point in the future.

Ten years ago this would have meant you would be recruiting for a job in management consulting, and perhaps that's true for you now. Perhaps you'll be interviewing with one of the world's most selective companies like McKinsey, Bain and BCG. However, it is just as likely nowadays that you'll be facing a case with a wide variety of top recruiters, (all similarly selective) including Amazon, Google, Microsoft, 3M, Fidelity and many more

For me, the situation arose when I had just started an MBA and wanted to get a job as a management consultant. There appeared to be a very big barrier between me and my dream job, and everyone agreed that this barrier was known as a case interview. I went to a lot of meetings of the consulting club, and people kept talking about cases. Sometimes they went further and started talking about some of the component parts of a case interview. Mostly in that respect they talked about something called a framework. It was very difficult for me to imagine exactly what they were talking about.

Based on that experience, I think I can imagine a lot of the things that are going through your mind.

What this book will cover:

Here's what I think you are (or should be) thinking about:

1. What is a case interview?

2. Why do recruiters use case interviews, and therefore what are they looking for when they give me one?

3. How do I get from my current position of not even knowing what a case interview is, to my ideal position where I am the zen master of case

interviews, so adept that I will shine in the interview and my dream employer will feel compelled to offer me a job?

My goal in this book is to address these questions.

Navigating through this book:

If you are just starting out on the journey and have the time, I'd suggest you read this book from cover to cover. I've deliberately kept it short and hopefully snappy, so that you should be able to zip through it quite quickly.

If, on the other hand, you are very time-crunched, and you have already started learning about cases, you may find it useful to go straight to the section which addresses your particular concern.

Early on, I'll provide some scripted examples of actual cases. Hopefully this will address that early problem of not even knowing what a case is. I've found that until you've got that issue out of the way, the rest of the theory doesn't really do much.

Once we've got a good baseline understanding of what a case is, we'll divide most of the rest of the book according to some of the major elements in a case, which are also the major things that recruiters are looking for. Those will be:

a) Structured thinking

b) Numerical analysis

c) Quality of thinking

You'll see these terms commonly occurring, as they are the major building blocks of a case interview.

Finally we'll look at how you can best use your time between now and your interview, including how to build the basic skills, how to move to advanced stuff so that you stand out from other candidates, and last minute prep items for when your interview is the next day.

Why do I feel qualified to teach you about cases?

I've spent a lot of time over the past ten years thinking about and working with these issues. First of all I was the MBA student described above – I muddled my way through learning and practicing cases, got pretty good at them, and after receiving a number of offers from top companies, I joined McKinsey & Company.

When I worked as a consultant at McKinsey, I chose to get involved with recruiting. I was trained in their techniques of how to create a case interview, how to run the interview, and how to evaluate a candidate. I really enjoyed the process and interviewed many candidates from all walks of life. I came to realize that a case interview is actually a very good way to test a lot of different things about a candidate. I also saw the difference between a candidate who was well prepared, and one who wasn't, as well as the big differences between a candidate who had what we were looking for versus one who didn't. In terms of preparation versus natural ability I concluded that everyone needs to prepare, but that in the end you also need ability as well as preparation (just as an athlete requires both natural ability plus training to excel).

Now I work as a career advisor at the Tuck School of Business at Dartmouth – one of the world's leading Business Schools. It's my job to think about case interviews pretty much 24/7.

Each year I work with about half of the MBA class as they prepare for interviews. I get a lot of opportunity to hone and test my thoughts on ways to help people learn about cases. Students at Tuck have a very high degree of success landing their dream job, and I hope that some of that is my influence. I certainly believe that in each part of my case interview journey; from student, to consultant, to interview coach, I've learned a lot about how to teach cases and how candidates can shine in interviews.

What do the experts say?

Throughout the book you'll see quotes that illuminate and hopefully add perspective to the topics being discussed.

As part of the process of researching and writing this book, I conducted over 30 interviews with successful candidates, interviewers and recruiters. They work at companies including McKinsey, Bain, BCG, Deloitte Consulting, Google and Amazon.

To preserve the anonymity of my interviewees, I will not attribute specific quotes to people or even to companies.

Every time I use a quote, you can be sure that it is representative of what was said by many of the interviewees.

What is a case interview?

A case interview (let's call it a case from now on) is a conversation based around a business situation in which the interviewer is evaluating a number of things about you as you have the discussion.

Most often, the case will be about a situation that you need no prior knowledge of. It's designed to be given to a large number of candidates who may come from a wide variety of backgrounds, and it's not designed to uncover their expertise, but the way that they think.

Specifically, a case is a way for an interviewer to see *how* you solve problems.

But wait a minute – how *do* you solve problems? That could cover a great many concepts. The way you solve a crossword puzzle is presumably very different from the way you settle an argument between friends, which is also very different from the way you might decide where to go on vacation.

Actually, there probably are similarities in the ways that you solve a great many problems you come across, but more importantly for our purposes there are definitely agreed-upon ways of problem solving that many businesses value and look for.

In other words, the case interview is testing the way you solve problems, but it rewards you if you solve problems the way the interviewer wants you to solve them.

> *"It's like a dance. That means you need to know the moves, and there's an expectation of a certain sequence and a way of doing it."*

So, as we go through this book, we'll learn the ways of problem solving that companies who use case interviews value. We'll learn the steps of the dance that they assume you have learned.

Some of these may be intuitive and familiar to you. Some of them will probably be new, and may not be the ways that you would choose to solve a problem if you were left to your own devices.

So what are these pre-defined ways of problem solving, and how does a case interview test them?

Rather than answering that question directly, I'll respond with another question (something that I learned as a consultant!)

What do Sherlock Holmes and Bain & Company have in common?

Have you ever read the Sherlock Holmes detective stories?

I love Holmes. Each case he solves seems so complicated at the start, yet is always reduced to a simple conclusion once Holmes has seen through the clutter.

Holmes remains one of the few popular heroes whose only power is his intellect and the logical way he brings it to bear. Perhaps that's why I identify with him so much, being a somewhat introverted, bookish person who if he is going to make a mark on the world definitely isn't going to do so in the world of sport or physical achievement! No, my best and only hope is to become known as a great problem solver!

Here's an excerpt from *Silver Blaze*, the first case in *The Memoirs of Sherlock Holmes*, originally published in 1894. The narrator and the first to speak is Dr. Watson, Holmes' friend and chronicler.

"I found myself in the corner of a first-class carriage flying along en route for Exeter, while Sherlock Holmes, with his sharp, eager face framed in his ear-flapped travelling-cap, dipped rapidly into the bundle of fresh newspapers which he had procured at Paddington. We had left Reading far behind us before he thrust the last one of them under the seat, and offered me his cigar-case."

"I presume that you have looked into this matter of the murder of John Straker and the disappearance of Silver Blaze?"

"I have seen what the Telegraph and the Chronicle have to say."

"It is one of those cases where the art of the reasoner should be used rather for the sifting of details than for the acquiring of fresh evidence. The tragedy has been so uncommon, so complete and of such personal importance to so many people, that we are suffering from a plethora of surmise, conjecture, and hypothesis. The difficulty is to detach the framework of fact—of absolute undeniable fact—from the embellishments of theorists and reporters. Then, having established ourselves upon this sound basis, it is our duty to see what inferences may be drawn and what are the special points upon which the whole mystery turns."

So what does this have to do with case interviews?

It turns out that the approach Holmes lays out is very similar to the approach that is required for a case interview.

In both instances, you take a situation which often looks complicated, and you deal with it by coming up with a simplifying model or framework, and then gathering and analyzing data to find out what is really going on.

The website of Bain & Company (one of the world's leading and most prestigious consulting companies) puts it more succinctly:

> *"You'll start by asking the right questions, and then dig deep into the numbers to unearth the right solutions"*

That's what the problem solving method as tested by a case interview is all about:

- Starting with a question that may at first glance seem complicated.
- Laying out a simplifying plan.

- Asking the right questions.
- Looking for the crucial facts.
- Unearthing solutions.

Not coincidentally, this is the way that many businesses like their people to solve problems. Whether you are going to work as a consultant at McKinsey or a product manager at Google, you will be required to deal with difficult problems by applying the above process. Indeed, if you can become a master of working the process, you will do very well in many different types of organizations (which is one reason why consulting companies like McKinsey and Bain are seen by many as excellent training grounds for future careers elsewhere).

Not a test of your knowledge, but of your problem solving abilities

If there's one concept that I want you to take away from this book, it's that the case is testing the WAY you think, not the information you've stored.

> *"It's a lot more about how you approach and think about the problem, than the actual answer you get to."*

This is such a radical departure from the traditional ways of being evaluated that I want to pause for a minute to explore this further.

Very often the types of people who find themselves facing a case interview are hard-working, clever, and driven to succeed. Very often they have achieved success in their life so far (whether in the classroom or in the workplace) by applying those attributes. They work harder than most of the people around them, they stick at it, and that, amplified by the fact that they are naturally clever, often gets them the result they want.

For instance, such people will often do well in school because they combine a work-ethic with intelligence and a natural aptitude to learn facts and re-use them so that they quickly learn how to succeed in tests.

As they get older, in many education systems the testing becomes more complex, and moves towards things like essays, papers, projects and so on, but really the underlying questions are the same – how much stuff do you know, how much time have you put into remembering it, and how good are you at regurgitating it.

All the way through the education system, and in some countries right through to the job market, this process delivers such people results. Good work delivers good grades. Good grades get praised by teachers and parents. Our hard-working, grade-getting students get into good Universities where they continue to get good grades and accompanying praise, and they graduate with good GPAs, good degrees, and (accordingly) good job prospects.

So far so good, right?

However, many such people hit a wall when they come to learning and succeeding in case interviews and it's the very skills and attributes that have brought them success so far, that they rely on in fact, that turn out to be their downfall.

Here's the problem:

A case is designed to be an opportunity for you to think through an issue you've never approached before, and to use certain ways of thinking to come to a conclusion.

It's specifically designed to see how you think on the fly, to find the candidate who can not only solve a problem they've never thought about before, but who actually enjoys that process and thrives in such a challenging and ambiguous setting.

Unfortunately, the way that most people approach the process of learning and practicing case interviews is to reduce them to predictable, learnable, memorizable facts and frameworks.

And this is a problem.

In fact it's a big problem.

That act of memorizing, of learning to rely on rote-learning, trips up many interviewees when it comes to the actual interview. It suppresses the natural ability to think on the fly. Instead of having a candidate in front of me who is smiling, relishing the new challenge, and enjoying the act of thinking, what I so often encounter is a candidate who is trying to force fit an approach from another case (or from a case interview book) that in reality both he and I would admit is not the best approach for the task at hand.

Never forget - the case is an opportunity to use your natural abilities and thought processes. When it turns into an exercise in you frantically trying to regurgitate something that you memorized for a case that is similar, but not the same as the one you're confronting, the results are that you do not shine. Intellectually you may get close to the answer, but in terms of the other qualities that the interviewer is looking for, you probably failed in the first twenty seconds.

It's unfortunate to say, but in truth many people who walk into a case interview would be better off if they'd never been given any advance warning of what the interview was going to be like. Many of them would be able to use their natural ability better than the skills they've learned in the intervening time.

Does this mean I'm advocating that you walk into what may be the most important and competitive job interview in your life without preparing?

No. I think there is a huge value in preparation.

But I think that you have to tread a fine line, to ensure that you are only ever enhancing your natural abilities, not smothering them.

I know that by now I am laboring the point, but I'll give one more summary –

Success in the case comes from the WAY you approach the problem, NOT THE ANSWER YOU GET TO.

There are many candidates who go through the right approach, demonstrating the right attitude and process to problem solving, who get the 'wrong' answer, but who end up getting the job. This is in contrast to the fact that there are a lot of other candidates who arrive at the technically correct answer, but do so in a way that is not in line with the behaviors or processes that the recruiter is looking for. Those people NEVER get the job.

OK, I'll stop laboring the point now. For a while at least.

Why do interviewers use case interviews?

There are some practical answers to this, and some philosophical ones. Let's start with the practical.

They do it because it works for them

Sounds obvious, right?

Many of the companies that use cases heavily are those that rely on their ability to hire the right person with the right set of skills, for instance management consulting. When your only product as a company is the intellect and quality of the people you send out to clients, you have to become very good at hiring the right people. The world's leading consulting companies have developed hiring the right people into a finely tuned science, and one of the key parts of that science is the case interview.

The fact that they keep using it speaks to the fact that they believe it works for them.

They do it because it works for other companies

There are a number of ways that 'best practices' in business get spread around.

First of all, they get copied. If somebody comes out with a better way of making a product, you can be sure that other companies who make a similar product will start to adopt a similar improvement.

Secondly, the vast majority of the world's leading companies have at some point hired consultants to improve their business processes. When you have a consulting company helping you design your talent acquisition process, and the consulting company believes that it is one of the world's experts on hiring the right people, then you can imagine that very often the advice ends up sounding a lot like 'do it like we do'.

Thirdly, most management consultants at the major firms do not stay in that job for very long. The average tenure at a major firm like McKinsey, Bain or BCG is around three or four years. Hence there are a lot of people leaving those companies. When a consultant leaves a consulting company and goes 'into industry' as they say, they will take a lot of what they have learned with them. One of the things they learn is how to interview.

Therefore you can never quite be sure when you go for a job at (pick your company), whether the person interviewing you used to be a consultant, or whether the company designed its hiring practices based on advice from, or based on imitation of, a consulting company.

Why are case interviews a good way to interview a candidate?

First of all, clearly a case interview is not the right interview style for every job. If I'm hiring a chef I might want to taste their cooking, or speak to people they've worked with in the past, or read their reviews. If I'm hiring a carpenter, I similarly want to see examples of their work. If I'm hiring a football player, I want to see how fast they can run, how they control the ball, how they fit into a team etc. All of the above examples are jobs that require a particular expertise, and for each one I will seek out actual proof of the expertise or ability.

Why do I mention this? Because actually a case interview IS a chance to evaluate your skills in a practical setting, very much like having a football player run with the ball.

A case interview is a way to test your ability to think through a question you've never thought about before. The reason you see it in use so often is that many jobs require people who can, without being told how, solve a problem they've never faced before.

To make the point, let's lay out a few sample jobs to explain this.

First of all, a job that does not require problem solving:

Working on a perfectly engineered production line.

I recently visited a manufacturing plant in Japan, the cultural home of efficient production lines. It was very clear that at every station (place where a person would work), a huge amount of thought had gone into making sure that the person in question would be confronted with exactly the same task, and hence do exactly the same action, every single time the next piece of equipment landed in front of him. The only reason a human being was doing the job was presumably because he was cheaper than a robot or more dexterous. In this situation, you are deliberately factoring out the worker's need to think.

As part of the factory tour, we were shown the recruitment tests that applicants had to go through, and they were literally practical tests to assess things like manual dexterity – for instance taking wooden pegs out of a set of holes and putting them into different holes.

A case interview would be a terrible way to recruit for this job.

What jobs DO require problem solving skills?

There are many jobs that require advanced problem solving skills. Sometimes it is because you are being asked to face a problem that literally has not been solved before, and in other cases the problem may not be unique, but you are expected to solve it without extensive support.

Often the tasks are unpredictable, and probably do not rely on memory or expertise.

For these jobs, there probably isn't a recognized body of knowledge, the study of which is a prerequisite for being allowed to practice the profession.

For instance:

Product Manager for an online retailer

Let's say you start in your role for a large online retailer, and you are responsible for building a business around selling a product into a new space (let's say you're going to pioneer the large scale online selling of carpets). As product manager, you will be given a lot of leeway to succeed or fail by yourself. There probably isn't a playbook for how you will approach this, and there won't be hundreds of years of industry best practice you can rely on. The reason you will be making a good income, better than the person assembling machines on the production line, is that you were hired for more than your dexterity.

Your job might involve the following:

(Without being told what to do or how to do it)

- Work out how, why and where people currently buy carpet.
- Find some parts of that process that could be replicated or improved online.
- Become an expert on sourcing carpets, including how long they take to make, how much they cost to ship and store etc., and work out how you will build your business (e.g., will you buy in bulk in advance and store in a warehouse, or will you simply be an intermediary between buyer and producer?)
- Get as good an understanding as possible of what major carpet retailers are planning in terms of online sales (you don't want any nasty surprises).
- Work closely with the team responsible for the actual look of your website, even though they probably have a far higher level of skill in that area than you do.
- Convince your boss to invest precious resources in your line of business, based only on your analysis and your confidence.

At some point in the above process, you will be one of the most knowledgeable people in the world about online carpet retail. Despite that, there will also be many times when you have to proceed with imperfect information, because there simply isn't a textbook or industry report you can buy. You will take risks, and you will make a great deal of decisions based on your judgment, not based purely on fact. Sometimes the decisions you make will not produce the result you want, and sometimes they will, and in both instances you'll learn from that experience.

Types of case interview

The term 'case interview' can actually cover quite a wide variety of interview questions and styles of discussion. At heart, they are all discussions based on a hypothetical situation. Some are short and snappy, and focus on particular sets of details; others are broad ranging and will seek to really uncover all of the issues in a situation.

At the short/snappy end of the spectrum we find the brainteaser or market sizing case. Sometimes this is a sub-section of a longer interview, and other times it will be the only case component you get.

Brainteaser/market sizing

A brainteaser type of case is essentially a math puzzle, and as with all cases seeks to test how you STRUCTURE a problem, what kind of ANALYSIS you do, the QUALITY OF THINKING you bring to bear, and the PERSONALITY that you reveal while you are doing this feat of mental gymnastics.

Some examples might be:

- How many apples are sold daily in the US?
- How many leaves fall from trees on an average October day in New England?
- How many bricks line the yellow brick road?
- How many gas stations are there in Texas?
- How many crisps are eaten in the UK every year?

We'll get more into the art and science of how to approach these later.

Classic case

The most popular case, and the one that we'll use in large part as our teaching model, is what I'll call the 'classic' case.

The types of question that you might be asked are very often in some way strategic, by which I mean there is a 'what should we do' component, but often include other areas of business as well, including marketing, operations, accounting, finance, pricing, people-management etc.

In fact, if you were to look at the curriculum of an MBA or other general business degree, you'd get a good insight into the types of areas that are fair game in a classic case interview.

We'll look at many such questions later on, but for now here are a few examples:

- A shoe manufacturer is looking at whether to enter the Brazilian market – what do you think they should do?

- A car rental company is experiencing a decline in profitability – what is going on and what should they do to remedy this?

- An ice-cream stand is thinking of introducing hot dogs alongside its cold offerings – is this a good idea?

- A Private Equity client is evaluating whether to buy a vineyard – what is your recommendation?

If the company that you are interviewing with has a particular focus, then you can probably predict that focus might follow through to the type of case they use, so for instance Amazon might focus on the areas around marketing and supply chain, whereas a pharmaceutical company might focus on R&D and pricing.

Blue Sky case

A variant of the classic case, but worth breaking out and looking at individually, is the 'blue sky' case. By this I mean it will be a simple enough business question, but the situation or product will be so novel or revolutionary that you will be forced to leave behind much of your current knowledge and rely heavily on your ability to think creatively. In my opinion, these cases are often used because interviewers find candidates too well prepared for 'classic' cases, and want to ensure that they can really see the interviewer thinking on their feet. Accordingly, blue sky cases might often sound provocative or crazy.

Some examples of blue sky cases might include:

- Our client has invented a teleport device. How much should they charge passengers to teleport from London to New York?

- A food manufacturer has invented a composting device that produces an output that is an edible soup. How should they market this?

- A clothing manufacturer wants to sell a type of floral dress to men in the US. How should it proceed?

- A drug company has developed a miracle cure for vertigo. How much should it charge for this drug?

- An airline is considering charging passengers to use the restrooms. What would you recommend?

While we develop this taxonomy, it's worth also considering the format of the case. Many of the above cases would be most likely to be delivered one on one, in a situation where you would likely sit in an interview room, using a notepad to take notes and do rough calculations when required. Let's call that the classic individual case.

There are other types of individual case you might get.

Paper-free

A variant on the classic would be the paper-free case. Again, this is often used in an attempt to get around the fact that many candidates are so well prepared that it is difficult to throw them off their game. So one technique that I see being used frequently is for the interviewer to say 'you don't need to write anything down, let's just talk'. This is also commonly used in non-consulting settings, with companies such as Amazon and Google.

Written case

A bigger difference, and the other end of the spectrum, is the written case. In this situation, you are given written materials (sometimes many days ahead of time, and other times at the beginning of the interview), and a question. Then you are given time alone to digest the materials, do the analysis, and come up with an answer. Sometimes your answer may be a written report, often in PowerPoint, and in other circumstances you will be asked to present your answer to one or more interviewers.

Group case

Finally, there is the group case. A common version of this is that you are placed in a room with a team of interviewees, and as a team you are given written materials, a case question, and a period of time to come up with an answer. If you have ever entered a case competition you will find this very familiar. The only difference is that usually in the group case there will be interviewers actually sitting in the room as you and the team go through the process. This creates a strange dynamic, where often you are working with the very people that in truth you are competing against, and the interviewers are not only testing your case skills, but also the way in which you work as part of the team.

Sample cases
Enough with the theory – let's see an actual example...

I think the best way to address this is to walk through an actual 'classic' case. I'll let you read through the script, and then afterwards we'll spend a while dissecting what we've just seen.

To set the scene, as with any interview you would usually arrive at a room with your resume and portfolio (containing some blank paper and a few pens or pencils). Alternatively you can also do case interviews via phone or video conference, with similar accessories.

In the room, after some small talk, you and the interviewer would start the case. The case would probably run around 20 or 30 minutes, although there are examples of much shorter 'mini-cases' and some could go on longer.

Example of a classic case

THE INTERVIEWER AND CANDIDATE, BOTH DRESSED FORMALLY IN SUIT AND TIE, SIT IN A SMALL CONFERENCE ROOM, WITH A LOW COFFEE TABLE BETWEEN THEM. THE INTERVIEWER HAS A PAD OF NOTES ON HIS LAP, AND THE CANDIDATE HAS A BLANK NOTEPAD OPEN ON THE COFFEE TABLE. THEY BOTH HAVE GLASSES OF WATER. THE CANDIDATE IS PERCEPTIBLY NERVOUS BECAUSE THIS IS AN IMPORTANT INTERVIEW, BUT DOES HIS BEST TO OVERCOME THIS.

INTERVIEWER

Our client owns a chain of restaurants in the Northeastern United States, and is concerned about declining profitability in one of the locations. What should she do to restore profitability?

CANDIDATE

OK, so just to ensure I captured this correctly, our client owns a number of restaurants, but only one of them is experiencing a decline in profitability?

INTERVIEWER

That's right.

CANDIDATE

And in terms of our objectives, has she given us a particular numerical target for profitability?

INTERVIEWER

Average profitability across the rest of the group is ten percent. She'd like to get the restaurant in question back to that level.

CANDIDATE

Great. Do you mind if I take a minute to think about how I'd approach this question?

INTERVIEWER

Go ahead.

THE CANDIDATE TAKES ABOUT 90 SECONDS TO DRAW ON PIECE OF PAPER THAT HE HAS LAID OUT IN LANDSCAPE FORMAT (ON ITS SIDE). HE DRAWS AN ISSUE TREE OUTLINING AT A HIGH LEVEL THE MAJOR AREAS FOR INITIAL INVESTIGATION, AND WITHIN EACH AREA HE MAKES SOME NOTES IN TERMS OF DETAILS TO EXPLORE.

WHEN HE IS FINISHED HE LOOKS UP, AND TURNS THE PAPER SO THAT BOTH HE AND THE INTERVIEWER CAN READ IT.

CANDIDATE

I've never worked in the restaurant business, but I've been to a lot of them as a customer, so it's really interesting to think about the way the business might work.

I think the first stage of this has to be a diagnosis of what the problem is, so for the first part of this discussion I'd frame the question as "Why is this particular restaurant experiencing declining profitability?" Once we've got a good answer for that I think we'll be in a good position to think of solutions. Does that sound like a good approach?

INTERVIEWER

Yes.

CANDIDATE

Great! So in terms of understanding what is going on to drive declining profitability, I've laid out a number of different avenues for us to explore. At a high level, when I think about profitability, I think of the interplay between revenues and costs. It could be that the problem is purely within one of these branches, or it could be a more complex interplay between the two.

I'd start with revenues, because when I think of a restaurant not doing well, I tend to think of empty tables. That's probably an oversimplification, and it may well not be the case here, but it seems like a reasonable place to start. So within revenues I've laid out two areas – one is that there may be a decline in the number of customers. The other is that the average spend from the customers may be reducing.

Before we dive in, I noted down a few thoughts in each category while I was thinking about them, so in the number of customers I think I'd definitely look at the absolute volume, but I'd also like to look at the breakdown in terms of time of day – perhaps there's a particular day or time of day that we're getting empty tables.

In terms of average spend per customer, there are really two branches I'd look at – either the actual prices are reduced in this particular restaurant, either via the menu prices or perhaps the use of coupons or other promotions, or the mix or volume of items ordered is going down, for instance people might be buying less alcoholic drinks, which I know from my own experience as a consumer tends to add a lot to the overall check! Or potentially some of the other... what I'd think of as 'upsell' opportunities from the waiter are not being chosen, you know how the waiter comes by after the main course and asks you if you'd like dessert? Or it may be simply that diners are choosing the cheaper main meals on the menu, for instance going for pasta instead of steak, or the equivalent for whatever type of cuisine this restaurant offers.

In terms of costs, I'd want to look into the main running costs of a restaurant to see what's changed recently, and particularly what is different compared to other restaurants in the chain.

For fixed costs, perhaps the rent has increased recently, or perhaps some other overhead costs like utilities. I think this is probably unlikely but I'd like to make sure.

For a restaurant, I'd imagine a key cost is staff, so again I'd like to look at the staff costs compared to the other restaurants in the chain, perhaps also looking at the proportion of these costs to the revenue. Perhaps the manager at this location isn't doing such a good job of optimizing the staffing levels, so we have unnecessary staff standing around, or perhaps it could be something quite complicated like healthcare costs or other benefits.

The biggest area I'd imagine for potential overspend in a restaurant is ingredient costs. Again I'd like to benchmark the costs against the rest of the chain, and compare them to dishes being ordered.

Finally, when I think of a restaurant kitchen I imagine a lot of food being wasted, although admittedly perhaps that's just based on my own experience cooking! I'd imagine there's a lot of room for variability in terms of how efficient the chef is, and also a lot of opportunity for being good or bad at predicting the right amount of perishable goods to buy on a daily basis. If you got that wrong you'd either run out of key dishes or you'd end up with a lot of unused fresh ingredients that you can't use the next day. And lastly, my sister works in retail and from what I've learned from her, a significant cost in that space is actually theft – either by customers or by staff. In a restaurant I'd imagine it's not the customers stealing meals by running off, although perhaps that could be true, but it's not unheard of for staff to steal from the business or under-represent revenues.

As I said at the beginning, I've never worked in the restaurant business before, so it's possible I've missed out something – have I got the key points or have I missed out something extra that I should consider?

INTERVIEWER

No, I don't think you've missed anything. Where would you like to start?

CANDIDATE

As I said, I have a hypothesis that the biggest driver for profitability in restaurants is number of customers, so I'd like to start on the revenue side and within that look at the number of customers. Before I do that, though, I'd like to check that with you. I think if this were a real client conversation the client may have a feeling for where the problem lies – either within revenue or cost. Do we have any direction from the client on this or should I just go ahead and investigate both avenues?

INTERVIEWER

We don't have any guidance from the client, but bearing in mind we only have twenty minutes to solve the case, I'd definitely advise you to focus your efforts on what you think are the most likely issues.

CANDIDATE

Great! Well, if this restaurant is experiencing declining profitability because of a decline in the number of customers, I'd expect to see a corresponding decline in customers. Do we have any information about customer volume over the period in question, ideally going back to before the decline in profit?

INTERVIEWER

I don't have any data on that, but I can tell you that actually the restaurant hasn't experienced a drop in the number of customers.

CANDIDATE

Oh that's interesting! So I was wrong in my initial hypothesis. OK, let's move on to the other side of the revenue equation. What I'd like to do is test my theory here that the average spend per customer is declining. Another way to look at this would be to look at total revenues to see if they've decreased relative to customer volume. Do we have any data either on average spend per customer or total spend compared to volume over the time period in question?

INTERVIEWER

Yes, we do have some data that the client's given us.

THE INTERVIEWER GIVES THE CANDIDATE A SHEET OF PAPER WITH A DATA TABLE

	2008	2009	2010	2011	2012
covers per week	200	200	200	200	200
revenue per week ($'000)	14	14	14	13	12

THE CANDIDATE TAKES THE PAPER AND SPENDS 10 SECONDS REVIEWING IT BEFORE TALKING

CANDIDATE

Interesting. So it looks like we've got information here going back for the last five years. We've got covers per week – what does that mean?

INTERVIEWER

Covers is a term used in the restaurant business to refer to number of customers.

CANDIDATE

OK, so we've got the number of customers per week, and total revenue per week. Interestingly, we can see that revenue has been declining even though, as you'd already told me, volume of customers has remained constant.

It would be interesting to work out the average spend per customer. Can I write on this exhibit?

INTERVIEWER

Sure.

CANDIDATE

So what I'd like to calculate is the average check size per customer. I'll start in 2008. We had 14,000 dollars in revenue per week from 200 customers, so I need to work our 14,000 divided by 200.

THE CANDIDATE TURNS TO A NEW PIECE OF PAPER AND WRITES OUT THE CALCULATION

CANDIDATE

We can make it a little easier by taking out some of these zeroes, which gives us 140 divided by 2, so that's 70 dollars average spend per customer.

THE CANDIDATE WRITES THIS IN A NEW ROW ON THE DATA TABLE

CANDIDATE

And that would be the same for 2009 and 10. And then using the same logic in 2011 we've got 13,000 divided by 200, which is 130 divided by 2, so that gives us an average spend of 65 dollars.

And then in 2012 it gets even worse. We've got 12,000 divided by 200 which is going to be 60 dollars per customer.

THE CANDIDATE TAKES A MOMENT TO LOOK AT THE DATA

CANDIDATE

That's interesting. I wonder what's causing that. It's particularly interesting bearing in mind the other restaurants in the chain haven't experienced such a decline, which leads me to think something's happened locally.

INTERVIEWER

What kind of things could have caused such a drop off in revenue?

CANDIDATE

Hmmm... if it were a drop in the number of customers I was going to say it might have been another restaurant opening and drawing away some of our customers. But what could be causing people to still come in but spend less?

If I go back to my initial structure, I can see I made some notes there... I wonder if there's been a change of staff. I know that whenever I eat out there's a discussion amongst the diners about whether to have another bottle of wine, or to have dessert, and I think a good waiter or waitress is able to have quite a lot of influence on that. So it could be staff changes. OK, before I get further into this let me just jot down some thoughts...

Let's think about some of the categories of things that might have changed. Internally to the restaurant or externally.

Internally we might have had a staff change, or maybe a menu change.

We've talked about staff changes, but within the menu we might have had an overall price change or it could be that certain cheaper items are more prominently displayed or are becoming more popular for a particular reason. We could include drinks in this mix, so perhaps there's been a drop off in terms of wine or other alcoholic drinks.

Externally, there might be something in the town that's caused people to spend less. It's not a national thing because then we would have seen it at other locations, but perhaps something happened locally, like a plant closure or something that is making people uncertain. Again, I feel that this would probably impact volume of customers rather than average spend.

Do we know if any of these are the reason?

INTERVIEWER

No, none of those things has been the driver. Could it be anything else?

CANDIDATE

(thinks)

Hmmm... What would make people spend less in a restaurant even though they're still coming in...? I think I've got the main possibilities but I do want to make sure I've thought outside the box as much as possible. So... this may be crazy, but it could be that there's a particular health drive going on in town which is driving people towards healthier meals. I know meals that are more vegetable-based rather than meat would probably be cheaper... although we've already talked about different ordering patterns... What else... I actually think that another thing that might drive less spending is if people are spending less time in the restaurant, so, this sounds really off the wall, but perhaps there's a curfew or perhaps... maybe we're getting more families who like to get their children home to bed early, or speaking of that even just having more families in general would drive a lower check.

I can't think of any more reasons.

INTERVIEWER

OK. What we found in this town was actually that a theater had opened downtown, and that was causing people to finish their meal early in time for the performance.

CANDIDATE

I can imagine! – rushing through the meal so you make the start of the performance, you're going to skip dessert, you're not going to linger for that extra glass of wine...

INTERVIEWER

Exactly.

CANDIDATE

Great. So now we know what the problem is, we can move into thinking of how to get that profit back up. Do you mind if I take another moment to jot down some thoughts?

INTERVIEWER

Not at all.

THE CANDIDATE TAKES 30 SECONDS TO MAKE SOME NOTES.

CANDIDATE

Here's how I'm thinking about this – there are a number of key categories I'd like to look at, and I've listed them in the order of priority in terms of starting with those most likely to move the needle.

I'd like to look at the following categories:

Timing

Pricing

Tie-ins with the theater.

I'd also like to try to put some numbers to some of the ideas as I go through them, to see if we can get back up to the $70 average check.

So... looking through these one by one, I think the easiest thing to do is to think about how we can get the diners who are going to the theater to arrive at the restaurant earlier. Perhaps we simply do this when they make the reservation, and we can advise them of a good arrival time. Perhaps we can give them some kind of incentive, like a happy hour, or perhaps let them know that the best parking spots outside fill up by a certain time.

Another aspect of timing is the speed at which we serve the meal. I've seen in some airports that restaurants make a promise to serve the meal within a certain time, so perhaps we could market this as a positive thing to the diners, that we'll guarantee to get theater-goers their meal within, say, twenty minutes. I think for either of these options, if we can get people back to ordering a full meal, with starter, dessert and drinks, then there's no reason why the average check size shouldn't return to normal.

Next is pricing. It may be that people who are going out to eat dinner and go to the theater are not particularly price sensitive, so perhaps we should just raise the prices. I'm not sure this would work, and I think that inevitably this would lower customer volume, so on reflection I don't think that's a good idea. I wonder though if there's something we could do – perhaps offer a suggested pairing that might go with the theater experience that might be a premium offering, perhaps a glass of champagne for instance. Let's see, if we're currently making $60 revenue per customer, we could suggest a glass of champagne that would probably cost more than $10. We'd probably lose some existing drinks sales, but perhaps that would net out at our target.

Finally, we could look at doing some kind of promotion with the theater. If we have a lot of crossover amongst our clientele perhaps we could push on that. Perhaps we could offer a discounted dinner to their patrons in return for them suggesting our restaurant at the time of the theater booking. In that respect then, we wouldn't be looking at increasing spend per customer, but rather increasing the volume of customers.

Or if the issue is that people are leaving without having a chance to have dessert, perhaps our chef could come up with some kind of dessert that would be appropriate for people to take with them and eat in the theater. We could also offer the ability to re-cork a bottle of wine so they could start it in the restaurant and take the rest home, which I know is popular in some places.

I'm trying to think if there's anything else I could come up with. I think I've got the main things but I want to see if there's anything really out of the box...

Hmmm...

OK. One last thought. How about if we run a special event every evening after the performance, so that people can come back to the restaurant after the show, have a final drink, and discuss the performance. We could perhaps invite cast members to dine or drink free, so people could feel like they're rubbing shoulders with the artists.

INTERVIEWER

That's great. So let's bring this to a close. Let's say the owner of the restaurant chain calls you up out of the blue, having not been following along with the work so far, and asks for a quick summary of what the answer is. What would you say?

CANDIDATE

Great. I'd say — You're losing money because of a newly opened theater in town which is causing your diners to spend less time, and less money, with you. The answer is to address this in a way that can restore spending, and we have a number of suggestions for ways to do this. We believe that the most likely avenue will be to encourage diners to arrive earlier, and also to commit to them that you can serve them a full meal in time for them to get to the theater. If we do this we believe we can return the average check size to $70 per diner which would restore profitability to your target of ten percent.

(pause)

INTERVIEWER

Great! That's the end of the case.

Analysis of the sample classic case

Let's take a minute to dissect what we've just seen, and from it let's aim to build an understanding of some common features of a case. Afterwards there will be a chapter devoted to each major feature, to really understand what the interviewer is looking for and how you can best prepare.

Opening:

The opening of a case is usually pretty standard. The interviewer lays out a question and then in essence 'hands over control' to the candidate. When I give someone a case question, I expect that either they will go quiet for a while and start thinking or may come back with some clarifying questions to enable them to better understand the situation.

One quick point worth making here – some candidates get the idea that they ALWAYS need to ask a clarifying question, but then if they don't actually have any question, they simply repeat back what I told them word for word, followed by 'is that right?'. Don't bother doing that – it's a waste of your time and mine, and it doesn't reflect well on you. In this case, the candidate gets pretty close to that, but I feel the way he emphasizes the question ("only one of them is experiencing a decline in profitability?") makes it work – he has seen something counterintuitive that probably has a strong bearing on the case and wants to check that he heard it right before moving on.

> *"Don't ask for clarification unless you missed something or you have a genuine question."*

Similarly, some candidates will have a thought pop into their head about the potential answer and will immediately ask it. For instance, in the example above, after being given the question a candidate might come back with "Is it something to do with customer volume?" As we'll see when we talk in more detail about structure, that may be the way you'd do it in conversation, but for a case you want to hold back on thoughts like that until you've taken a moment to organize them, either on paper or in your head.

In terms of objectives, it is quite common to find out if there is any numerical or strategic goal, but again you should only do this if it is not clear from the question. Quite often the question itself means we have already described the objective. So for instance, if the question is "a sportswear company wants to know whether it should enter the China market", then I think it's reasonable to assume that an objective for this case is to get to an answer on that. Don't get too hung up on checking in with me if our goal is profit or market share unless it would materially drive the case (if you think about it, in most cases we can assume that there needs to be profit).

One good reason to ask questions in the opening is if you realize you don't know enough about the industry or the way that the company in question works. This isn't uncommon – cases can be based on some pretty obscure settings. And if you don't understand how this business works, it is very difficult to have a sensible conversation about it.

In this case, it's absolutely fine to admit that you are new to this industry, and to ask for some information. Here's what some of the experts said on the subject:

> "Often you'll get a case and you really don't understand the industry and how it works. How can you talk intelligently about something you don't even understand?! In my experience it's absolutely OK to ask the interviewer. Here's how I did it – I'd say something like 'I don't have a good understanding of how this industry works. Let me walk you through how I think it works, and then perhaps you can help me fill in any gaps"

> "If you don't understand the business, it's OK to say something like 'I'm not familiar with this industry, could you please give me some understanding of the business model?'

The final part of the opening is for the candidate to ask for a while to think. Out of the whole case interview, this is perhaps the most 'false' in terms of this being a simulation of a business discussion, and at first it can seem very uncomfortable. It is, however, a convention of the case interview, so don't be afraid to ask for a minute, and then please go ahead and take your time to go quiet, think through your approach and take some notes. The interviewer may watch you, but more likely will check their email or gaze out of the window!

> "It's a great time to calm and compose yourself. Use this minute as the ignition for the case."

Structure:

If you look at this example, the candidate takes a while to jot down some thoughts, and then describes a 'structure' or 'framework' that he has put together. In this case he has noted down that he wants to explore two main areas – revenues and costs, and within those areas, he has further developed some ideas on what he wants to analyze. We'll talk a LOT more about structure in the upcoming chapter, but for now let's just say that this is a major component of the case. As Sherlock Holmes observed, coming up with a framework of facts enables you to then find out where the problem lays. The way you organize that framework shows the interviewer a lot about the way you think, and quite frankly signals a great deal in terms of how successful the interview is going to be. If, after taking that minute to think through the issue and make some notes, you can come up with something that shows you have a pretty good plan to cover the relevant issues, you will be a long way towards success.

> "Think of the structure as a table of contents. It's a good opportunity to show your breadth of thinking."

> "Structure is a road-map to think about the problem. It gives you an organized way to think about how you'll approach solving it in a systematic fashion. It makes you seem thorough, and it makes the interview seem more like a professional piece of work."

Let's take a minute while we're here to observe the way the candidate describes the framework. This is a good example of where business communication is slightly different from natural conversation. The candidate first of all tells the interviewer that he has two high level areas of focus: "At a high level, when I think about profitability, I think of the interplay between revenues and costs", and then he starts to flesh out revenues, before returning to costs. This way of communicating – first of all describing the major 'chunks', before diving into details, also takes a little practice. It's a lot more natural to simply dive into the first one without ever even naming the other chunk(s).

A final (and critical) observation about the way this candidate's lays structure. It is tailored to the question at hand, and shows the interviewer that the candidate is aiming to solve this specific question, for this specific situation. It sounds obvious, so let me describe the alternative that I so often see.

Bad example:

"When I think about a business I think about a number of areas. Macroeconomic trends; what's happening in the market; what's happening with customers, and what's happening internally. Internally I would look at fixed costs and variable costs."

Does this sound like something you'd say if a friend or colleague asked you to think through an issue of a restaurant losing money? No. But trust me this is what more than fifty percent of candidates will sound like once they have 'learned' how to do case interviews.

Why?

Because they have memorized 'useful' frameworks that can be applied to a large number of situations.

Then they have regurgitated one of those frameworks, with no attempt to use the language or specifics of the case.

Remember, the interviewer (or the company) has chosen to do a case interview specifically because they want people who can think for themselves, NOT because they want to employ people who unintelligently memorize then regurgitate facts or frameworks. Starting out with something like the above will almost definitely get you dinged in the first minute. You'll run through the rest of the interview thinking it's going fine, but you lost it as soon as you started talking.

> *"It's immediately apparent to me if someone is trying to use a structure they learned from a book. The words they use, the order they use, it will be the same as about fifty percent of the other candidates that day. I understand why it happens, because everyone's prepping using the same one or two books with the same prescribed formulas. I'm not against people preparing – that just shows they're taking this seriously – but they have to realize they can't just trot this stuff out in the interview and expect to succeed."*

As I said, we'll cover this a lot in the chapter on structure, but it's such an important issue that I wanted to get it out there straight away.

The main body of the case dips in and out of the next two qualities that are being tested – Analysis and Quality of Thinking:

Analysis:

If structure is the art of laying out your plan of attack, then analysis is following the plan and actually investigating everything you said you would investigate.

Analysis can sometimes be simple and high level and consist of merely talking through the questions you have in mind and getting answers to those questions.

At a more detailed level, analysis will often involve using numbers to answer your question. For instance, in this case the question is "are customers spending less than they used to?" and we find the answer by looking at historical data on number of customers and revenue per week. In other words, in this case the interviewer has buried the answer beneath a level of data and then you as the interviewer have to do the job of digging into the data to uncover the insight.

Analysis, then, has two major components:

1. Asking the right question

2. Digging for the answer (often using data)

We'll look at these in a lot more detail in the chapter on analysis, but I'll cover a few FAQs here before we move on, in large part because these are things that get a lot of people very stressed.

Q. Will there always be data?

A. No, many cases are purely discussions, with no data provided. But you should always enter a case interview assuming that you will be working with numbers, and until you are given clear guidance that there is no data, you should ask for it if it would be useful to answer the question you have in mind.

Q. Will I be expected to do complex math in my head?

A. No. Companies and interviewers know that in the real world you will use a computer to do your calculations, so they are not looking for math machines. On the other hand, it is a convention of the case interview that you will not use a computer, so that means that if there is math to do, you *will* need to do some calculations on paper. The majority of the calculations I see are at the level of what my 10 year old daughter is currently learning at school – perhaps simple fractions, perhaps a long division or two, probably percentages. So if you feel uncomfortable with this level of math on paper, then you should start brushing up your skills.

Quality of thinking:

We've looked at the fact that to navigate a case you need to be able to lay out a structure, an organized way of thinking through a problem, and then work your way through that structure, asking the right questions and getting the answers.

Is that all we observed from the example?

I'd argue no. If you simply laid out a good structure and then walked through it, you might end up sounding quite robotic. Let's be honest, a computer could probably do that, and the company does not want a computer to do your job (that's why they're interviewing you, and that's why they're not simply giving you an exam that involves selecting the right structure and then doing analysis.)

Take a look back through the script and you'll see some good examples of a number of elements we can group under the category Quality of Thinking. These elements are:

1. Business Sense

2. Judgment

3. Creativity

Let's go through them quickly one by one, and then we will spend a lot more time on them in the chapter on quality of thinking.

1. Business Sense

I said at the beginning that a case is designed so that you don't need knowledge or expertise of the situation in order to succeed.

But in reality we all carry with us a lot of knowledge. Think of all the books and articles you've read, all of the programs you've watched, all of the millions of things you've observed in your life.

A case interview is a great opportunity to show that you are the sort of person who loves collecting knowledge and who most importantly loves using it.

For example, our candidate makes the observation that in the restaurant business a failing restaurant is often the result of not enough customers. This isn't rocket science, but it's well worth observing. It shows that this candidate likes to think about business situations. He has probably sat in a restaurant where there weren't many customers and wondered how on earth the restaurant is still in business. If you asked him, he'd probably be happy to share his observations on the kinds of things that successful restaurants have in common. In short, this is someone who observes what is going on around him and who likes making use of that knowledge. That sounds like someone I'd like to hire.

There are many other examples of knowledge in the interview. Some of it is subtle, like the terminology that our candidate uses. Words like 'upsell' and 'fixed cost' show that he has at some point been exposed to some business concepts (perhaps simply by reading the business pages of the newspaper) and is happy to use them.

He also uses his knowledge to come up with sensible assumptions. For instance, he knows that a glass of champagne is probably more expensive than another type of drink that a restaurant would serve. He doesn't need to be an expert, but simply be willing to draw on his experience and bring it to bear.

2. Judgment

I do many hundreds of case interviews in a year, with MBA students, undergrads, PhDs, military officers, doctors, and people from many other walks of life. They're all clever, hard-working people. I bet that in normal life they draw on their judgment frequently, and I bet that in general it serves them well.

Strangely, when it comes to doing a case interview, many people leave their judgment at the door, which is a huge shame.

Let me say more about this.

So far we've learned that you need to listen to the question, come up with a structure that will allow you to investigate all of the possible options, and then work your way through the structure doing analysis that will reveal to you the final answer.

Many people take this to mean that they should, at all times, remain completely non-judgmental about what the likely answer might be, and should always reserve their judgment until all of the analysis is done.

That's all well and good in theory, but in reality it makes it sound like you either have no judgment, or that you are afraid to express it. Neither of which you want.

Let's use our example.

"I'd start with revenues, because when I think of a restaurant not doing well, I tend to think of empty tables. That's probably an oversimplification, and it may well not be the case here, but it seems like a reasonable place to start."

This is a great example of using judgment.

A bad example would be:

"In order to look at profitability we need to look at both revenues and costs. Where would you like me to start?"

Think this through – which one of the two people above would you most like to hire for a position where most likely they will need to use their initiative and judgment on a daily basis?

But as I said, something happens during the process of learning cases that turns people who are normally very happy to use and share their own judgment into people who are terrified to express an opinion for fear of either being wrong, or because they think it doesn't fit with the idea of using a structured approach.

3. Creativity

We all know creativity when we see it. It's the ability to make something that wasn't there before. That something may be a picture, a song, a product, or even just a thought. It's not easy, and society places a very high value on individuals who exhibit this skill. Obviously at the far end of creative endeavor you get artists of many types, but back here at the business end of the spectrum there is still a huge demand.

Where did we see creativity in the example case?

Actually there are many examples. I'd argue that as the candidate lays out his structure, he uses a number of creative techniques to populate his structure with content. For instance, he imagines himself in a restaurant. He also draws on experience from other areas when he mentions that his sister works in retail, thus he is able to bring insight from one industry to another.

The most obviously creative part of the interview is the part towards the end when the problem has been identified, and we get to generating solutions. That probably mirrors real life and real work. It's usually relatively simple to identify a problem – the bit that requires creativity is coming up with a solution. In this example the candidate starts with some 'sensible' solutions such as increasing prices, and then moves forward into more 'out of the box' thinking such as inviting the actors to have a free drink after the show.

You might argue that this thinking is not truly creative, in the sense that a true artist might come up with something well and truly out of the box. Fair enough. If we need to modify the term creative to something like business-creative, then so be it. Think it through. The job probably requires somebody who can bring enough creativity to get over the hurdle, but not so much that their ideas are crazy and unworkable. So if an artist had gone through this interview and come up with something incredibly creative (let's say he suggested we rip off the roof, put sand on the floor and have people eat in swimsuits because people tend to spend more when they feel like they're on vacation!!), then he would have nailed the creative part but you can be pretty sure he wouldn't get the job – nobody wants somebody so crazy that they won't fit in with what will probably be, by and large, a sensible job in the real world.

Giving the summary

Along with the part at the beginning of the case where you take a minute to go quiet, the summary is another convention that is probably different from reality.

The convention is that you are meant to pretend that you have actually done the work and investigated the issues in enough depth that you can give a confident summary. In fact, the things they are testing are your ability to speak clearly and confidently, as well as being able to summarize a complex issue in 20 or 30 seconds.

Take a look at the script. The candidate could have talked about many of the things that were discussed in the case, but deliberately kept to the most relevant. He knew that brevity was a virtue at this stage. He also kept it quite confident, despite the fact that he was probably really thinking "hey, we've only scratched the surface of this issue, I'm sure in reality it's a lot more complicated than this and I'd need to do a lot more analysis to be able to confidently advice any particular course of action."

Example of a market sizing case

Other than the 'classic' case, there is one more type that is common enough to be worth our while going through a scripted example. This is what's known as a market sizing case.

A market sizing case tests the same things that a classic case does, albeit with less analysis and in less time. Such a case will usually take less than 5 minutes, and may very often be a part of a larger classic case. It's an easy way for an interviewer to get a candidate to do some math without having to provide any data up front. It's also a particularly good way to test another competency – comfort with ambiguity, which we'll talk more about after the example.

INTERVIEWER:

How many ride-on lawnmowers do you think are sold in the US each year?

CANDIDATE:

That sounds like an interesting challenge! I have to admit I've always wanted to drive one of those things but I've never lived in a house with a yard big enough to justify one.

Do you mind if I take a moment to plan my approach?

INTERVIEWER:

Please go ahead.

THE CANDIDATE TAKES THIRTY SECONDS TO MAKE SOME NOTES ON THE NOTEPAD IN FRONT OF HER.

AT THE TOP OF THE PAGE SHE WRITES THE QUESTION: # OF RIDE-ON MOWERS BOUGHT IN US PER YEAR. SHE THEN UNDERLINES PER YEAR TO REMIND HER OF THAT FACT.

CANDIDATE:

OK. I've got some thoughts on how I could approach this, do you mind if I run you through the logic before I run the numbers?

INTERVIEWER:

No, that sounds like a great approach.

CANDIDATE:

OK, so I'm going to look at this in terms of households, starting with the number of households in the US, and then using a number of filters to try to get to an approximation of the number of households in the US who might use a ride-on mower. Then I'll need to remind myself that we're looking for the number sold per year, not in use, so I think I'll need to make an assumption about the average life cycle of a mower. Finally I think I'll have to add on another amount to account for the professional user such as groundskeepers and freelance yard workers.

Does that sound like a good approach?

INTERVIEWER:

That sounds great. And I think we can restrict ourselves to simply looking at home users, without having to worry about professionals.

CANDIDATE

Great! That should simplify things.

THE CANDIDATE MAKES NOTES AS SHE SPEAKS, AND DOES QUICK CALCULATIONS WHEN REQUIRED.

So, I think I'd start with the number of households in the US. I think there are around 300 million people, and if we assume the average household has 3 people, then that gives us around 100 million households.

Now, I'm trying to think of some logical subdivisions that would get us closer to the answer. I think the first one is whether someone lives in a city. If they do, they probably don't have a lawn and therefore don't need a mower.

I don't know the exact percentage of people in the US who live in cities, but let's say 40%. So that leaves us with 60% of our 100 million households, which is 60 million households who live in suburban or rural areas.

Next I'm going to say that even in those suburban or rural areas, not everyone lives in a house that would have a lawn. Some may still live in an apartment. So let's bring that 60 million down to about 45 million.

So that gives me a very rough approximation of the number of suburban and rural houses in the US.

But I'm still not there yet. If I think of the town where I grew up, certainly not every house had a lawn big enough to need a ride-on mower, and then equally even for those with a big lawn, not everyone did their own grass cutting.

So first of all, out our 45 million houses, let's say that only 10 percent of them have yards and lawns big enough to justify a ride-on mower. If I think about my home town, that seems about right. That gives me a total of 4.5 million. And let's say that half of those actually do their own mowing – so that brings me now to 2.25 million.

So I think we could reasonably expect around 2.25 million ride-on mowers to be in use in the US. So the big question is how frequently you need to buy one. I think it's a bit like a car, and there you'd have some people who'd replace it every three years, some people would hang on to it for a long time, and of course some people would actually buy or sell it used. Which is an interesting point. Are we calculating the number of new models sold or should we include used models as well?

INTERVIEWER

Let's do both.

CANDIDATE

OK, good. How can we think about that?

(THE CANDIDATE TAKES A MOMENT TO THINK)

I wonder what proportion of mowers out there are new compared to used? How could I calculate that?

Let's see… thinking through the life of an example model. Let's say it's bought new, and the original owner keeps it for 5 years, then trades it in or sells it privately to buy a new model. That used model will now get bought by someone else who may keep it going for another 5 years. Does that sound right? Maybe the people who buy the used model would keep it going longer, but then maybe they might pay less on annual maintenance. Let's pick an average of 5 years before it reaches the end of its practical life. So that would give us a 50/50 split amongst new and used for the mowers that are out there.

So actually each type – used and new has in effect a 5 year turnover. If we divide our 2.25 million by 5 then that gives us approximately… 450, 000 mowers sold each year, half of which are new and half of which are used.

Let's see… does that sound reasonable…

How could we sense check this?

Well, approximately 500,000 mowers means around 250,000 new mowers. Per state that would mean about 5,000 new mowers sold. If an average state has 100 retail outlets, then each outlet would sell 50 per year. That seems reasonable. I know if I think of the Home Depot near me they have about 20 mowers parked out front but I don't know how frequently they make a sale. So, yes, I think that's reasonable.

Analysis of the sample market sizing case

Let's think through some of the major elements of what we just saw:

Establishing an approach:

With a market sizing case, the trick is to work out exactly how you're going to get a number. In this case, the candidate realized she would need to find the number of households using a ride-on mower, and then work out how often they'd purchase such a product. To get to the target number of households, she started with the total number of households and then devised and applied a number of filters. This is known as a top-down approach, where you start with a large number (often the population of a country) and use a number of filters to refine that number.

The candidate could have got a similar result by doing a bottom-up approach, starting with an individual household and then working out how many such households there might be in one town, then how many towns in the US.

Crucially, what this candidate did well was to lay out the initial approach and then check in with the interviewer. This is a great way of making sure you're on track and perhaps getting some pointers.

Using multiple steps:

As an interviewer I get nervous when someone makes a big leap in the numbers. What I mean by that is if you went from the total US households and then tried to guess in one step that about 5% of those households lived in rural houses with property large enough to need a ride-on. There are too many elements involved, and there is too much sensitivity to how accurate your assumption is.

If you can insert a number of sub-filters, then each one requires you to give a little extra thought to each assumption. Sometimes it is no more scientific, but it feels better. Most of the time, though, you really do get a better result.

Remember, you are not being tested on the final number; you are being tested on the approach you take. If I hire you to run a long and complex process, I want to know that one of the first things you'll do is make a plan which breaks that process up into manageable chunks.

Making very broad assumptions:

The element of the market sizing case that people find most difficult is making assumptions, often based on little or no information or expertise.

Actually, an interviewer will usually design such a case so that most people can have some kind of opinion on the assumptions. Hence this case is about lawn mowers. Even if you've never used one you've probably heard of them, and can be reasonably expected to think through the kinds of things that might drive ownership and purchase.

The key here is to use your judgment, and to communicate frequently with the interviewer. The candidate in this example does a good job. First, she always makes a suggestion at a number, and then she frequently tries to justify that by referring to an observation. For instance, "out of 45 million houses, let's say that only 10 percent of them have yards and lawns big enough to justify a ride-on mower. If I think about my home town, that seems about right." The fact that she has made the effort to link her assumption to an observation will get her credit.

If your assumption is so wrong that it risks throwing off the whole calculation, your interviewer will usually let you know. So as you go through the process, keep a careful eye on their reaction. If they look doubtful after you have offered an assumption, it's OK to check in with something like "Does that sound reasonable to you?" But don't get to the point where you are asking permission for every single step. That sounds like you might turn into an employee who needs constant supervision, which is not what they are looking for.

Rounding:

When you are doing a 'back of the envelope' calculation, it's always acceptable to round your numbers – first of all it allows you to move faster, and second it's a good way to remind yourself not to start trusting too much in your assumptions.

I'll give you an example by way of explanation:

Let's say we are trying to calculate how many families in the UK will go to Disneyworld in Florida this summer:

Population of UK is approx. 60M

Assume 3 per household = 20M households

Assume 70% households have had children at some point (any age) = 14M

Assume 15% of those have children of Disneyworld age = 15% x 14M = 2.1M

Assume 75% of those would like to go to a US Disney park once during childhood = 75% x 2.1M = 1.575M

Assume 75% will choose Florida over California = 75% x 1.575M

As you can see from this – we are making calculations here that seem very precise. We're now talking about 75% of 1.575M. It may be tempting to do that calculation if only to show that we embrace math and are good at it, but I'd suggest that it would be foolish to do so because it gives us an unreasonable sense of security in the number. We'd be far better off admitting that by now we have made 5 separate assumptions, all of which based on little or no information, and thus whether the answer now is 1.2 million or 1.181 million is far beyond our ability to judge. Frankly we can only be confident with our number to within, I'd say, half a million.

So when you find yourself getting into what seem like very precise numbers, ask yourself - how confident are you about the trail that's led you to that precision? If you actually don't believe you could say you are right to that level of accuracy, let the interviewer know that, and let the interviewer know that for that reason you will round the number.

Sense-checking:

We've already talked about how, for each assumption, it's a good idea to see if you can ground it in some kind of observation.

Equally, when you get to the end, it's always worth taking a moment to ask yourself if what you've ended up with sounds reasonable. Sometimes it's literally a matter of asking that. Other times, like in this example, you could try to come up with another test – another quick calculation that would enable you to look at the number from another angle. Even as you set out on that, the interviewer may well cut you off – he won't care that you get a new or better number, he'll give you the credit for at least testing it.

Case interviews test a combination of skills

In our dissections of example cases, we've surfaced quite a number of different skills that were being tested.

It's highly probably that any one of those skills could have been tested in a better way.

So what does that tell us about the case interview, and the kinds of jobs it is used for?

I think it tells us that the case interview is a technique that you use when you want someone who does well at a wide variety of competencies. In fact, I'd go further and say that the case interview tests for a fairly rare confluence of abilities – the ability to think logically, to be able to do complex analysis, to think creatively, to have confidence in your own judgment, AND to have good enough people-skills to come across as enthusiastic and genuine in the midst of a fairly stressful job interview.

Hopefully you feel that you'd do well in such an interview. If after reading this introduction you want to run screaming from the room and bury this book in the back yard, you should take a while to reflect on that – maybe the job that interviews in this way isn't a job that is going to be a good fit for you. I'm not trying to put you off. Far from it – I think that if you are going to succeed, then it helps to have a good understanding of what skills you have, and why you believe you'd be superb both in the interview and the job.

The key thing to realize is that doing a case interview is not like taking an exam. Even though it can sometimes feel like it, this is not a situation where the answer that you come up with will win the day. In fact, it's the opposite. The 'test' that you are taking is actually a personality test, and the various intellectual hoops that they make you jump through are in many ways just attempts to get you to show your true personality.

They want to find someone who is:

<u>Friendly</u>, and who can start to build a relationship with the interviewer.

<u>Enthusiastic</u>, and who seems to genuinely enjoy the interview (if the interview is a simulation of the job, then it stands to reason they want to hire someone who'd enjoy the job).

<u>Collaborative</u>, who is able to work with someone else to get to the right answer, rather than feeling like they need to do it all themselves.

On the flipside, here are the types of behavior that case interviews often bring out in people:

(Reminder – these are personality types to AVOID!!)

Not interested in the other person in the room – the candidate will treat the interviewer merely as an instrument of the test, and will spend most of their time focusing on the paper in front of them.

Unenthusiastic – often sighing audibly when presented with a tough challenge, frowning, shaking their head etc.

Argumentative and, worse, combative – someone who wants to prove they are right, regardless of the effect it will have on the other person, and who feels that any criticism of their ideas is a personal attack.

I'd argue that the candidates in the scripted examples do well on all of the positive elements above. Even though we can't see their body language and the expressions on their face, they do a lot with language to convey both their enthusiasm and their collaborative nature. Take a look through the scripts to see if there are any tips you could take away to help with your own case delivery. Sometimes something as simple as saying "great!", or "interesting!" can make a big difference.

To conclude this section, I'll give you two contrasting quotes. Both are real quotes that I've heard during the recruiting process:

> *"I'm sure I made a lot of mistakes during the case, but I felt that I got on really well with the interviewer – in fact we spent such a lot of time talking about our personal interests that we ran over our allotted time."*
> CANDIDATE (who got the job)

> *"He scored brilliantly in every technical dimension – his math skills were off the chart and his structure was perfect, but there was no way we could hire him, he was just so unfriendly and impersonal. I'd never in a million years want to put him in front of our client."*
> RECRUITER (talking about someone who didn't get the job)

Now we've addressed the immediate question of what exactly a case looks like, let's go back through the major components in more detail. We'll cover:

1. Structure

2. Analysis

3. Quality of Thinking

For each chapter we'll look at the following topics:

- What qualities are recruiters looking for, and why?
- What does good performance look like?
- How to practice

4. Game Plan

Finally, we'll spend time on developing a game plan for your preparation, so that you can be sure you are approaching case prep in a structured and orderly way that is going to have the best chance of success.

Structure

Simply put, having a structured conversation entails first of all laying out a plan of the things you want to talk about, and then using that plan to shape the ensuing discussion.

> *"When you start with a problem, you could take it a thousand different ways. The structure helps you cover everything and work through it methodically."*

> *"If you're given a problem, you should have a systematic way of working through all of the possible parts and factors. You should understand all the moving parts, including how they interact; and you should be able to communicate all of this easily. All of this is just as important in day to day business as it is in the interview."*

What does unstructured thinking look like?

Before we get into how to come up with a structure, let's start with the opposite – what does unstructured communication look like?

If I asked you to think through a business situation that you'd never approached before, how would you even start? Almost any business situation worthy of discussion would not be a simple yes or no, and would not be solved by simply exploring one single set of issues.

It's tempting in the face of such a challenge to pick the first thing that comes into your mind, dive into it, get the answer to that thought, and then move on.

Let's say I asked you to help me to decide whether to replace my home's oil-fired heating system with a wood-fired furnace.

To give you some background to this issue:

Where I live in Northern New England, most houses are heated by some kind of oil-burning boiler or furnace (a boiler heats water which then circulates heat around the house through pipes, a furnace heats air which is then blown around the house). Fifty years ago when many such homes were built, oil was dirt cheap in the US. Now it's very expensive, plus it's not very environmentally friendly especially if you consider it is probably brought from somewhere a long way away like Texas.

Many people are replacing their oil burning heating source with something that burns wood. Wood is a plentiful fuel in the heavily forested North East. It is thus a lot cheaper than oil. Whether or not it is better for the environment to burn wood than oil is hotly debated. Some say that cutting down trees is the last thing we should be doing, others say that trees are a renewable resource, because every time you cut one down, another one grows up in its place pretty quickly.

Finally, there is a practical consideration of space and ease of use – burning wood requires a lot of effort moving it around. Wood is heavy and it takes up a lot of space. The boiler itself then needs a lot of space, and maybe needs a more advanced chimney. Plus the boiler is very expensive and requires an expensive installation, so even if you saved money on the fuel, it might take a long time to recoup the investment in the equipment.

As you can see there are a lot of issues, and this is not a straightforward question for many people.

A typical non-structured conversation, and probably the conversation we'd have if neither of us were consultants and we were in a social setting, might go as follows:

1. Wood is cheaper than oil. And that's only going to get more so. Oil is a finite resource so it's never going to get cheaper, although all the innovation with shale sands seems to be discovering new supplies all the time.

2. Oil is politically precarious and its price goes up and down depending on what's going on in various parts of the world. It seems like we're never far from some kind of turmoil especially in the Middle East.

3. Burning wood is not good for the environment. You cut down trees, and then the smoke from the fire releases a lot of carbon, plus there are many particulates in wood smoke that are not good for people. In major cities in the old days when everyone had fires, buildings were blackened by the smoke and people got very ill.

4. Actually some environmentalists think burning wood *is* great for the environment. Once a tree is grown, its carbon is going to get released back into the atmosphere one way or another – even if you just leave it to die and fall over it will release its carbon. Then once you've cut it down, another tree will grow in its place, and in doing so will absorb a lot of CO_2. Compare that to burning oil – that's an outright addition to the CO_2 in the atmosphere.

5. At least wood comes from a local source if I live in a forested area, so if I want to be green I should think about the transport costs of oil too. Plus it's a good idea to support local industry. Every time you buy local firewood you are supporting local families who depend on forestry for their livelihood – rather than giving money to big oil.

6. Aren't those wood fired furnaces pretty big? Do I have space for that? I heard that you need a large area in your basement to store the wood and move it about. Plus wood's pretty heavy. I'm not sure I want to be carrying around stacks of wood every day. And what if I went away on vacation – would I need to get someone to come into the house to keep the boiler going? If not, my house would freeze.

7. Don't wood fired furnaces put out lots of smoke? How would my neighbors feel about that? I can just imagine how pleased they'd be if I was putting out a constant plume of dirty smoke. Although I've heard that many new wood burners hardly put out any smoke, or is that just marketing?

8. Did we cover the politics of oil in enough detail? What about tax credits for renewables. What if they go away?

And so on.

What you see from the above is that a 'regular' conversation probably starts with one of the key drivers and then makes its own way. Sometimes thoughts follow logically, sometimes there are leaps, and sometimes we circle back to something we were talking about earlier.

In actual fact, what we've just done is a good example of what it's like listening to a client, or someone who is stressed and thinking through an issue. Somebody in your company or your client might already be thinking about the issues, but without the power of structured thinking they never get beyond a constantly evolving list of issues and problems. Because of this the situation feels too big to deal with.

Some of the most effective consultants and business leaders I've worked with have really honed the skill of listening to a 'brain dump' like the one above and then summarizing by saying something like:

> "Ok, so from what we've discussed, it sounds like there are three major questions we need to answer: First, is a wood-fired boiler going to be more expensive or cheaper than your current oil boiler? Second, what are the environmental advantages of switching? Third, are there any other major considerations, such as ease of use? If we can answer all of those, then we'll be in a good position to make a decision on whether this is a good move. Have I got that right, or is there anything we've missed?"

If we were to try to write out the elements of the above conversation in a structure, perhaps as a preliminary step in a case interview, or otherwise as the start of a project to solve the issue, we might come up with something like the following:

1. Costs – what are the main costs of a wood furnace?

- The main cost we're looking at is the fuel cost – is wood truly cheaper than oil? Are we including all the hidden costs of transporting and stacking it? Do we think costs of inputs are volatile or stable?
- The other main costs is equipment - so what is the purchase price? Installation? Maintenance? Let's compare these to a traditional oil-fired furnace.

2. How can we break down the environmental impact?

- The main one seems to be pollution from burning the fuel. Wood seems like it would create more smoke – is this a bad thing? Can we quantify how bad? Is there research or existing opinion we should look at?
- The second issue is sustainability – is it sustainable for the planet to keep burning oil? How about wood? Do we believe that our wood would be harvested from a forest where new trees would subsequently grow?

3. Finally, let's talk about other issues – did we miss something important?

- The biggest one is mileage of fuel, although this probably comes into environmental factors as well – is it better to use a locally sourced product or one that has to come from a distant country?
- The second is space – do we have the space in our house to house the equipment and store the wood?
- Thirdly, let's talk about personal preference – am I excited by the idea of stacking, carrying and burning wood or do I want the convenience of the oil furnace clicking on whenever it is called for?

Why is structure useful when approaching a difficult problem?

Bringing a structured approach is useful because it makes the problem seem **manageable.**

In addition, laying out the main categories makes it easy to **check for gaps.** For instance, comparing the summary above with the client's list of questions might reveal a gap in terms of regulations or laws that might stop us. So the client might respond to the consultant that there is probably a fourth category and that could be incorporated into the work.

Having an upfront structure also allows you to **plan the time and resources you allocate** to the upcoming work or conversation. Even if it is just for a discussion, you can remind yourself that there are several key areas, all of which are equally important, and that you want to spend, for instance, ten minutes on each. If you don't do this, you might forget the last issue and by the time you get to it you will have run out of time.

Finally, the work ahead is now **easy to communicate**, both within the client organization and to any other consultants who may be working with on the project.

The reason I'm sharing this is because I want you to understand that coming up with a structure to answer a question is not an abstract test. It is a skill that consultants and business leaders use that has real, practical value.

> *"When you present a proposal to management, you're competing against other people for resources, so you've got to be able to show you've really done your homework. Structured thinking is not just an academic exercise, it's a way of building an argument and showing you've done all of the right analysis."*

> *"The reality in most business situations is that you're trying to create a compelling argument for change. If you don't consider every alternative, you'll get torn apart."*

If it helps, think of the structure in this case as a project plan, because a lot of business activities, including the type of problem solving that might be used for strategic decisions, are essentially projects, by which I mean they are a set of activities designed to achieve a certain goal, executed in a deliberate and organized way.

To summarize: there are many advantages to using a structured approach to problem solving:

- **It makes the problem seem manageable** – rather than an overwhelming collection of thoughts, now you have a defined set of issues.
- **You can plan your time and resources**, and break the work, or the conversation, down into discrete sections or workstreams.
- **It enables you to check for gaps** – you can quickly ensure you're covering everything and thus ensures that important things are not missed.
- **It's easy to communicate** - so if somebody comes late to the conversation (or project) you can quickly show them what is going on.

Why is structured thinking useful in the interview?

In the interview, taking a minute to lay out a structure has a number of additional benefits, which are closely linked with the real-world benefits.

1. By having an upfront plan you don't get distracted by the first thing that comes into your mind.
2. You can take a minute to review the plan in collaboration with the interviewer with the goal of ensuring that you will cover all of the relevant angles.
3. You can quickly and easily communicate the plan to the interviewer and perhaps get feedback to help you iterate and improve it.

How to create a good structure

OK, so we understand the need for structure, but how do you come up with a good structure, especially in a stressful interview, when you have been given about a minute?

This is something that takes practice, and is probably the most difficult part of the case to master. The good news is, once you've got the hang of it, you're well on your way to overall success.

We'll cover the following areas as we develop our understanding and ability:

- **Techniques for developing a structure**
- **Design principles to bear in mind**

Techniques

So - you hear or read the case question, and you know that in the next one or two minutes you'll have to talk the interviewer through your structured approach – your plan for answering the question.

So now what? How do you come up with a structure?

When you're starting out – this is a big issue, so don't worry if right now it seems insurmountable. Trust me, it's a skill that everyone picks up and once you get going it gets easier.

So how do you start?

Let's first of all not do this in real time. This is one of those skills that you have to learn in slow-motion before you ramp it up to full speed. It's like learning golf. You need quite a few hours of practice on the elements before you put it together and head out for a full 18 holes.

Let's look at an example:

Initial question:

Our client is a large supermarket chain in the US, considering launching an online grocery delivery service. Should they go ahead?

What goes through your head in the next ten seconds probably approximates the various issues that the client is thinking of. Your thoughts might fit into the following areas:

- Reasons why the answer may be yes or no
- Complications – things that mean this is far from being an easy yes or no
- Gaps in your knowledge that would need to be filled before you could provide an answer
- Things that you think you might know but that you need to check
- And probably many more types of initial thoughts, many of which might come at you in a jumble.

Step one – get your thoughts down on paper

So, the first step is to get these down on paper – you can do it in list form, or you can space them out all over the paper like a mind-map. The key is just to get them written out without censoring your thoughts.

Why don't you take a minute and try it? On the next page I'll show you some of the thoughts I came up with but I think the learning experience will be greatly enhanced by you going through it as well...

Did you get a bunch of ideas? Good!

Here is what I came up with:

- Delivering heavy groceries would be expensive, presumably this is why Amazon hasn't already dominated this market?
- Do we have to maintain a fleet of delivery trucks, or would we partner with a shipping company?
- What about our competition? Are they planning or already doing anything similar?
- Do our customers want this? How much would they pay for this service?
- Would our customers spend more per order or less?
- What would it cost to get this up and running?

It turns out that my thoughts have come out as questions, which I often find a useful way to get into a case. But it's not essential. You could also have notes such as:

- Cost of delivery
- Method of delivery – buy, build or partner
- Competition
- Customers – willingness to pay
- Customer spend – increase or decrease
- Start-up cost

Step two - grouping

The next step is to look at our thoughts and try to group them.

For now, let's try to come up with titles for the groups, but don't get too hung up on that.

For instance, we might have a group called customers

We might also have a group around competition.

Then there might be a group around the logistics, such as transportation, picking (getting the orders from a shelf or warehouse into grocery bags)

In an ideal world you want to end up with somewhere from 2 to 4 groups. More than 5 is not manageable.

Step three – add a hierarchy to your groups

What do I mean by a hierarchy?

A hierarchy involves us getting used to a way of expressing our structure that sorts things out not just according to groups, but within those groups allows us to sort things in terms of whether they are high level or detail.

You will have noticed so far in this book that I very often use bullet points to show a hierarchy of ideas. At its most simple a bullet hierarchy might look like:

- GROUP TITLE 1
  - Detail a
  - Detail b
  - Detail c
- GROUP TITLE 2
  - Detail d
  - Detail e
  - Detail f

For our example then, we might end up with:

- Customers
  - Do they want this service?
  - How much would they pay for delivery?
  - Would they spend more or less in each shop?
  - Would we get more loyalty as a result?

- Competitors
    - Who are the main competitors?
    - Do they do anything like this already or are they planning to?
    - How would they react to us if we launched this?
- Logistics
    - Delivery model
    - Fulfilment center
    - Staff
    - Leadership
    - Web infrastructure

It is often appropriate to go for a second level (a lower level in terms of hierarchy) of sub-details. As you get practiced at creating these structures, you will get used to breaking down details into sub-details as you go. For instance, initial thoughts might include:

- Customers
    - Do they want this service?
        - Are they already asking us for it?
        - Could we survey them to find out if they'd want it?
    - How much would they pay for delivery?
        - We could ask them?
        - We could look at equivalent services such as Amazon
        - Presumably this would be a reasonably low price – would it be worth our while?
    - Would they spend more or less in each shop?
        - When people buy online they may feel like it's not 'real money' and thus spend more
        - On the other hand, a lot of our in store purchases are impulse buys, would we lose out on those online?

- o Would we get more loyalty as a result?
  - If we were the only major supermarket offering this, would we improve our customer retention?
  - How much is customer retention worth to us?
- Competitors
  - o Who are the main competitors?
    - Are any other major supermarkets doing this in the US? Elsewhere?
    - What are Amazon's plans in this space?
  - o Do they do anything like this already or are they planning to?
  - o How would they react to us if we launched this?
    - Would we force others into this space and thus end up with a situation whereby everyone has to offer online delivery even if it turns out to lose us money?
    - Would smaller competitors be able to compete – maybe we'd drive some of them out of business?
    - Would larger competitors be able to do this cheaper and faster than us?
- Logistics
  - o Delivery model
    - Do we need to own and maintain a fleet of trucks?
    - Who else could we partner with?
  - o Fulfilment center
    - Would we ship from a warehouse or from the supermarket?
  - o Staff
    - Do we use existing staff or do we need more?
    - Are there special skills required?
  - o Leadership
    - Do we have any senior managers with any experience of this area of business?

- Do our senior team have the bandwidth to launch a major new initiative like this?
  - Web infrastructure
    - How much would this cost?
    - Are we experts?
    - How long would it take to get it up and running online?

How do you know if you've got the right categories?

When you start out, you will worry about whether or not there is the perfect structure. When you are working fast and going by your instinct, of course there will be times when you end up going down a path that is different from the person before you or after you.

In fact, having done cases with many hundreds of people, what I've seen is that people always converge on the right ideas. After all, the ideas above are probably pretty sensible, and most people would probably come up with them.

Where there can be difference is in the names and types of categories, and this is OK.

For instance, we could approach the above question through the high level categories of Pros and Cons.

We could also approach it through the high level categories of Financial and Strategic. After all, most business decisions come down to a simple calculation of whether it will make money or not, and then are sense-checked (sometimes even over-ruled) by strategic issues. By this I mean that sometimes a company will invest in a project that initially loses money, with the belief that it will have a long term benefit such as driving a competitor out of business or eventually creating a demand.

Either of the above alternative structures would allow us to investigate the issue, as would my first version.

I can also reassure you that if you come up with an interesting new spin on a question, the interviewer is more likely to be intrigued than put off. Imagine doing a case with twenty people in a day. If most of them use the same structure that can sometimes get repetitive for the interviewer. I'm NOT suggesting you deliberately use an off the wall structure just to prove you are in interesting person, but I AM suggesting that you go with what makes sense to you, without worrying too much about whether you've got it spot on.

One more comment about nailing the right structure – this process is very much akin to the way a company will lay out an actual project. I've been in many of those scenarios where the discussion about how to lay out the different workstreams and questions goes on for days, with countless reiterations on whiteboards, powerpoint, etc. So don't feel like the professionals get this right first time either.

Design principles

As you come up with groups and details, there are a number of useful design principles that you can practice. You can use them initially as you come up with your structures, and you can also use them when you are giving feedback on other people's structures during case practice.

1. Order of priority

2. Equivalence

3. Mutually Exclusive

4. Collectively Exhaustive

Order of priority

> *"We're looking for people who can prioritize, and a case is a good way to test for this."*

As you draw out your structure, try to place the most important group at the top, and then go in descending order of importance. It doesn't matter if it turns out you are wrong about what is important or not, what matters is you use your judgment.

For instance, for the supermarket case, we might look at our emerging structure and decide that the most important thing to find out is whether it is logistically feasible. After all, if it is impossible to do, we are wasting our time deciding to try it or not.

Very often you will see financial issues up top. As I said earlier, many business decisions start with 'can we make money' and then run through supporting issues.

Equivalence:

What I mean by this is that things in a certain level of your hierarchy should be roughly equivalent in terms of type and scale.

Let's look at groups that are not equivalent by looking at a new case:

Example question: Should I open a pizzeria on Main Street"

GROUP 1 – REVENUES (How much money would I generate from selling pizzas?)

GROUP 2 – COSTS (How much would I have to spend to make the pizzas?)

GROUP 3 – WEBSITE DESIGN (what should it look like?)

I would argue here that website design is not as much a high level group as revenues and costs. If this is what I'd got after my initial brainstorm, I would try to think what high level group website design could go into. Perhaps Marketing?

That would give me:

REVENUES

COSTS

MARKETING

I think that would be better. It may not be perfect, because you could argue that marketing would go under costs, but perhaps we want to keep it split out because we believe that a new restaurant would live or die by our ability to get the word out.

Once you're happy that each of your groups is reasonably equivalent, do the same with details.

MECE – Mutually Exclusive and Collectively Exhaustive

MECE (pronounced Me See) is an acronym that was apparently coined by McKinsey. You may hear it used by other case interview candidates.

Let's look at each of these in turn.

Mutually exclusive:

This is probably the most critical design component of a good structure – namely that you should come up with groups that are not subgroups of each other. Revenues and Costs are nicely mutually exclusive – it is difficult to think of something that both costs and makes you money.

There are a number of other common groups that work well with Mutually Exclusive:

- Internal
- External

- Short term
- Long term

- Domestic
- International

As you can see from the examples, it's easiest to be sure you're mutually exclusive when you have opposites. You can probably think of a lot more.

Another way to think of mutually exclusive groups is to group by stage in a process. For instance, if you were to look at ways to improve customer fulfilment by an online retailer you might group by stage:

- Customer places order online
- Item is selected and packed at warehouse
- Package is transported from warehouse to customer's home

The great thing about a process flow is that it is usually impossible for an item to be in two places at once, hence you can be sure you have got mutually exclusive groups.

At other times, however, you may come up with categories that are not strictly exclusive but may still be worth using. A few times already in this book, we've seen examples with costs and then another category of things that probably actually would come under costs. In such an instance you have to use your judgment. If the case will truly hinge on net profit, then you should probably include all factors that cost money under costs.

However, if there is another driver, such as the desire to be good for the environment (such as with the wood boiler example), or the need to build a customer base (as with a pizzeria on main street), then you may keep the relevant group split out from costs.

If you feel conflicted, a good way out of this is to pick one way, go with it, and then explain to the interviewer that you know your structure is not truly mutually exclusive but explain why you have laid it out as you have.

Collectively Exhaustive:

Collectively exhaustive means that when you add all of your groups together, you haven't missed out anything.

This one is useful, but beware, because for many people it turns out to be a wild goose chase (meaning they think it is more important than it is). When you have purely opposite groups, it is easy to be collectively exhaustive. For instance, once we've got INTERNAL and EXTERNAL, we can be sure there isn't another state of being out there that is equivalent.

For other sets of groups, however, it is often the case that the two or three we come up with are the most relevant, but there's no way we can be sure we've covered everything. There are two ways to deal with this:

1. Either have a group called 'OTHER' or 'MISCELLANEOUS'

2. Get used to the idea that your structure may not be collectively exhaustive, and that's probably OK. If required you can even tell the interviewer that you believe there may be other factors but that you'd like to focus on the most important ones.

I prefer option 2. It shows that you are willing to use your judgment and that you are not a slave to an acronym.

A final thought on MECE – use it as a guide to help you draw your structure, not as a rule. Because of the fact that so many candidates get hung up on it, a number of experts I interviewed expressed doubts about the value of MECE, as demonstrated by the colorful quote below:

"MECE is about as helpful as a sack of hammers! People would be better served by making sure they've got a generally sensible structure that aims to capture the different possible answers to a broad problem."

Take ten seconds to look back at your structure:

Once you've got your structure, take another ten seconds in the interview (or a few minutes in our slow-motion practice world), to review what you've got.

Here are some questions you could ask of it:

- If I follow this plan will it probably get me to the answer?
- Is there anything I've missed (within reason), that couldn't be inserted into my structure and that might turn out to be a major driver of the answer?
- Are the component parts of my structure reasonably comprehensive?
- Are the component parts reasonably mutually exclusive?
- Are levels of hierarchy reasonably equivalent?

Describing your structure to the interviewer

Once you've reviewed your structure, you're ready to describe it to the interviewer. Now it's easy, because you're simply narrating what you've noted down. Note that this is the first time the interviewer is really going to hear from you, so it's the point at which they will probably make a significant first impression about whether you are going to succeed in the interview or not.

Note also that if you are doing a phone interview, this stage becomes even more important, because the interviewer can't see your beautifully laid out notes, and if you don't describe them correctly he will assume you haven't got them.

So – how do you narrate your structure to the interviewer?

Firstly, it's not a matter of simply voicing the words on the page. You've probably got it in note format, and that's not going to sound too compelling. Aim to put it back into business-style language, and wherever possible insert small examples of you using your judgment or knowledge.

To repeat - *Simply reading out your structure as if it were a shopping list is not going to impress anyone.*

Here is a good example of how you might read out your structure for the 'online delivery model for a supermarket' question.

"OK, this is a really interesting question, and as a consumer who has to travel to the supermarket every weekend and spend an hour or so traipsing around the store, I would really appreciate this. In fact, I used to live in England where Tesco and the other major supermarkets have launched this in a very big way, but I realize that's a much smaller country with more population density.

In order to come up with an answer for whether or not our client should do this, I'd like to look at a number of high level categories – customer demand, competitor action and reaction, and logistics. I think if we cover these we should have a good understanding of the key drivers. Have I missed anything major?

I'd start with customer demand because if nobody wants this service then I think the rest becomes a moot point. So first of all, do customers want this service? Perhaps they're already asking us for it via online or in-person feedback, or perhaps we've done, or could do, surveys to gauge the demand. Of course, a key question we'd also need to answer is how much they would be willing to pay. I'd imagine that if this were free, most if not all customers would say they'd like it, whereas if it is too expensive nobody will want it. We might even be able to come up with some kind of demand curve which would predict how many customers would use the service at different price points.

In addition to asking our current customers, we might get some data on this by looking at other benchmarks, such as the price that people pay for Amazon delivery.

The other key question I'd like to look at regarding customers is how much they'd spend per shop. I know that a lot of the success of a supermarket comes down to attracting customers to spend more than they'd intended while they browse up and down the aisles. If they were to shop online, I'd be worried that they'd stick to the essentials and we'd lose out on a lot of potential revenue. On the other hand, I know that masters of online sales like Amazon are great at suggesting extra purchases, so perhaps we'd be able to do that.

Finally, with regard to customers, I'd like to look at whether launching such a service would significantly increase customer loyalty. I'd imagine that actually many shoppers are already loyal to a particular store, because there is a lot of cost in terms of learning a new layout for a customer to go down the road to another store, but on the other hand there are probably some customers who do follow the bargains week by week. If we could retain some of them that might be a significant advantage. I wonder if there's a way to put a revenue value on this in the way that some companies are able to calculate the lifetime value of a customer.

My next major category is competitors. I'd like to get a sense of the landscape in terms of who else is out there – who are our major supermarket competitors, are they doing anything like this and if not, do we have any intelligence about their plans. Then of course there are the major online retailers like Amazon. What are they doing – how much money are they making etc. Some of this we have to use assumptions for because I'd imagine that such competitive information is not readily available.

I'd also look at potential reactions of competitors if we did this. Would they rush to join us, and if so is that good or bad for us? Perhaps this would really be an advantage we could use to drive some of our smaller competitors out of business. On the other hand, what if someone else does it better than us, and then we find ourselves even worse off than when we started?

Finally I'd want to look at the logistics of actually doing this. It's great coming up with an idea, but we need to check it's feasible to implement. The first image I have in my mind is of a number of delivery trucks zipping about the neighborhood. Of course there are already a number of companies like FedEx and UPS that do this, but I suspect that they'd be too expensive for us, so it might be that we'd need our own trucks, and then drivers etc.

The other image I have is of a fulfilment center. When I was studying for my MBA I visited one such center and it was a very impressive facility with miles of conveyor belts and people rushing around. But in England I know that the supermarkets who did online delivery actually picked the items from the supermarket shelves – perhaps that would be the better model. I'd like to explore this in more detail in terms of the pros and cons of each.

We also need to ensure we have the right staff with the right skills. I don't imagine it would be a problem to find drivers or item pickers but I'd like to make sure. Probably more importantly, do we have any senior leaders with experience in this field, and if not can we hire some? We might need to use a headhunter to attract someone from a major online retailer. We should also make sure that our leadership team have the bandwidth to take on such a major project. Finally I'd like to get an understanding of how easy it is to launch such an online site. I presume it's mostly a matter of cost, because I think there are a lot of website designers and online retail experts in the world and we'd need to hire a team and get them going.

I think if we looked through all of these factors we'd be in a good position to answer our client's question, so I'd like to start by diving into customers in more detail..."

What if your mind goes completely blank?!

The above process relies on you having a lot of initial thoughts, which you can then group and categorize.

But what if those thoughts just aren't flowing? It does happen sometimes, particularly in a stressful situation like a job interview.

If you do find yourself in this unfortunate situation, here are some tips that may help. Not all of these will work in every situation, and some may suit your way of thinking more than others.

Remember – these are suggestions, not rules.

Think in questions

What major questions do you need to answer in order to be able to solve the case? Often these major questions are along the lines of:

- Is it a good idea?
- Will it make money?
- Can our client do it? Is it the best thing for them to do right now?

Look for what's changed

Very often we are dealing with a change in an otherwise stable situation. For instance, a company has started to lose money, or a particular branch has reported something unexpected, or a product is selling better or worse than before.

If I told you that for the last three years my journey time to work had been ten minutes but recently it's been taking me twenty minutes, your first question would probably be "what's changed?"

Asking this of yourself and perhaps directly to the interviewer can often get you going.

So let's look back at the case with the restaurant where one branch is losing profitability:

- What's different about this branch?
  - Internal
    - Staff? (volume, quality)
    - Menu? (choices, prices)
  - External
    - Macro trends (local employer closed down?)
    - Competitors?
- Can we fix the difference or do we have to adapt our business?

When faced with 'what to do', think in terms of 'either X or Y'

For some reason I find myself using this frequently. Perhaps it's the way I'm hardwired. If you asked me to think of ways to grow the audience for a theater in New York, I'd probably start by thinking of binary splits.

By this I mean… We could EITHER focus on our existing audience, getting them to come more, OR we could try to get new people in.

Once I'd started down that line of thinking I might grow it out to something like:

- New audience
  - Geography
    - Expand our advertising to the suburbs
    - Work to attract tourists
  - Age
    - Perhaps widen choice of shows to appeal to different age groups?
    - Discounts for old and young?
    - Family passes?
    - School trips?
  - Socio-economic group
    - Advertise in different places?
    - Different types of show?

- Discounted tickets (how to stop cannibalization of current revenues?)
- Existing audience
  - More spend per visit
    - Raise ticket prices?
    - Increase prices or volume of concession sales?
  - More visits
    - Increase frequency of new shows
    - Loyalty program

Another very common binary split would be INTERNAL or EXTERNAL.

For instance:

- How could a hospital Emergency Room cope with increasing demand?
  - Internal
    - Add capacity
      - More space?
      - More equipment?
      - More staff?
    - Increase efficiency of capacity
      - Increase throughput capacity
      - Reduce waste
    - Reduce demand
      - Divert some patients and procedures elsewhere in the hospital
      - Build a new unit in the hospital to take lower levels of emergency
  - External
    - Add or use capacity elsewhere
      - Work with other hospitals in the city/region to spread demand

- Re-route ambulances to most effectively use system
- Build 'out of hospital' centers
  - Reduce patient demand overall
    - Educate patients about what they should use the ER for
    - Public Health campaigns to aim at long term health improvements

And one more that I find very useful is COULD/SHOULD.
This reminds us that some business decisions might in theory be a good idea, but in practice might not be best for our client:

E.g.,

- Should our client launch a burger restaurant chain in India?
  - (COULD) Is a burger chain in India a good idea (regardless of who does it)?
    - Is there more demand for this product than is currently supplied?
    - Could we increase demand?
    - Can burger restaurants make money in India?
  - (SHOULD) Is this the best thing for our client to do?
    - Does our client have specific skills in:
      - Burger restaurant chains
      - Launching in new countries
    - Does our client leadership have the bandwidth to oversee this?
    - Does our client have the financial resources to do this?
    - Are there any other major opportunities that would be better?

How to ensure your structure is tailored to the question

A structure that is tailored to the question is ALWAYS better than one that has been memorized and regurgitated.

> *"I started case prep by memorizing structures, but it was counterproductive. Later on I learned to design my own frequently used structures that I could fall back on."*

As we've seen, structured thinking is a key component of most case interviews. It is one of the elements that you will be 'graded' on, and it is probably the least intuitive and least close to the way you would naturally run through the conversation had you not been taught.

Therefore it is the area that causes the most amount of anxiety for people as they learn how to do cases. To address this anxiety, there are a number of case interview books that promise to teach you formulas for how to come up with the perfect structure, or framework.

Unfortunately, because case interview books that teach a certain type of framework have become so popular, many candidates walk into the interview room having learned the same 'secret formula'. This leads to two logical outcomes. The first outcome is that any interviewee who actually tries to use a framework that they learned from a popular book instantly fails to convince the interviewer that they are capable of using their own judgment to come up with a tailored solution. The second logical outcome, as a reaction to the first, is that firms have started to come up with more imaginative case questions that demand a tailored response.

I believe that learning suggested frameworks is an excellent way to *start* your case practice, and indeed many thousands of successful candidates have found such case interview books valuable. But I also believe that it is essential that by the time you walk into the actual interview, you have internalized the suggested frameworks to the point where you can draw on them as thought-starters and then create your own tailored version.

"I want to see you improvising a coherent plan on the fly. It's OK to be drawing on stuff you remembered, but be sure to 'personalize it' to the case as you write it down and talk me through it."

So how can you achieve tailored structures that do not look like they have been dragged up from your memory?

Practice

The best way to learn this ability is to practice it. The good thing about practicing structures is that you don't always need to go through a full case with a partner to get the value. You could just as easily replicate the exercise we did above – take a question, give yourself a couple of minutes to jot down a structure, then take a while to 'pressure test' it.

Pattern recognition

Once you have done a lot of case questions, and come up with a lot of structures, you will probably start to notice some very common themes. For instance, you'll probably come across a lot of cases that are about assessing profitability. There will also be many more that are about acquiring or divesting companies, or pieces of a company.

As you start to notice these patterns, I'd encourage you to look for the common themes among the structures you are using. Perhaps they will be identical, or perhaps they will be merely similar.

Find what fits for you

Once you notice the elements that are being repeated for a type of question, you could probably come up with your own 'cheat sheet' of the types of structure you find yourself using and the elements you find yourself including in these.

If you do this (and I encourage you to do so), bear in mind that you must ALWAYS be answering the question that the interviewer gives you, not the case you did last week (and certainly not the case that you did from the book that everyone else is using!). Sometimes you will be able to use your 'go-to' without changing it, and other times you will need to tailor it.

> *"Get away from the canned structures. Whether you lay it out as a tree or not is irrelevant, as long as it looks neat and we can both follow it. Remember, the structure is for you as the interviewee."*

The main thing I hope you take from this discussion is the fact that structured thinking in a case is not an exact science.

In fact, the thinking process that you go through as you come up with your own structure is exactly the point of a case interview. If a company wanted to test your memorization skill the interview would be designed very differently.

Don't be afraid to take the time to think, and don't be afraid to make changes to your structure as you start to lay it out or as you walk through the case. It's this kind of flexibility that is required in the job.

Similarly, as you go through the case, there will be other times when it may be appropriate or useful to come up with a new structure. That's great. The more times you take a moment and jot down some kind of structure, even if it's as simple as 'pros and cons', the better.

In fact, it may often be the case that partway through the case it's relevant and useful for you to jot down a new structure. We saw it in the scripted classic case, where the candidate was asked for ways to increase revenues. He started to come up with ideas, then caught himself being unstructured, and laid out a number of high level categories. This mid-case structuring is a great practice to get into. It proves to the interviewer that you are truly a structured thinker, compared to the many other candidates who give the initial structure and then revert to a style more akin to stream of consciousness for the rest of the discussion.

Practice drills

You can come up with any number of case questions for yourself and then practice drawing out a structure as described above. A good source of issues is the financial pages of the newspaper – perhaps look at a headline, try to come up with a business questions behind it, draw out your structure, and then read the article to see if you missed anything.

> "The key for me was developing the skill of working out what kind of issues I'd want to investigate for a given problem. I'd practice by opening up the newspaper, picking a business story, and then thinking through what kind of issues I'd want to understand to get to the bottom of it."

To get you started, here are a number of case questions:

- A hospital is experiencing long wait times for patients to get seen by a doctor in the emergency room. What should it do?
- A private equity firm is considering buying a company that makes ice cream cones. Is this a good investment?
- A packaging company is considering buying a major manufacturer of cardboard. Is this a good idea?
- A toy company that makes high quality model trains is considering entering the China market. Should they?
- The owner of a food truck wants to increase his profit while maintaining sales volume. How could she do this?
- A fashion designer wants to launch a line of clothing made out of paper. Is this a good idea?
- Worker productivity at a tractor plant is down – what could be happening? How could we fix it?
- A company has developed a car that runs on solar panels that are built into its roof. How much should it charge for this car?
- A mail-order clothing company is considering dropping the smallest size for all of its T-shirts. Is this a good idea?

- A supermarket has noticed that profits from ice-cream are dropping. What should they do?
- A friend of the family is thinking of opening a luxury furniture store in your home town. Is this a good idea?
- You feel that you are spending too much on groceries and restaurants. How can you decrease the amount you spend on food?
- A state governor wants to encourage more innovation in her state. What should she do?

Numerical Analysis

Remember the excerpt from Sherlock Holmes that I shared earlier? I actually cut a small piece out as it wasn't relevant to the discussion at the time. Here it is:

> *"We are going well," said Holmes, looking out the window and glancing at his watch. "Our rate at present is fifty-three and a half miles an hour."*
>
> *"I have not observed the quarter-mile posts," said I.*
>
> *"Nor have I. But the telegraph posts upon this line are sixty yards apart, and the calculation is a simple one."*

Why do you think the author included this? It doesn't help us understand the case at all.

I think it was included to impress us – to demonstrate how clever Holmes is and also to show how intellectually agile he is. Not only does he solve crime, he can also do math!

In those days, people had to do math in their head. They didn't have computers in every pocket. So think how much more impressive it would be nowadays if you could do an equivalent calculation – it would demonstrate a lot about you:

1. You are good at math (obviously)!
2. You have the mental agility to understand HOW to do the calculation, and what calculation to do.
3. You are confident in your abilities, and happy to use numbers whenever they can provide useful insight.

And if you did such a task in a stressful situation, for instance during a job interview, I would add a fourth:

4. It shows that you are able to do difficult things under pressure.

If you consider the above pieces of insight into your skills and personality, you can understand why a recruiter might want to throw a math problem at you during an interview. In fact, point 1 (proving your actual math ability) is probably the least important.

Therefore, very often a case will include some kind of quantitative analysis. At the most basic this may be you interpreting a chart, and at the most complicated it may involve you doing a multi-stage calculation.

In all instances that I've come across, this math will be done without a calculator or computer. However, it will not need to be done in your head - you may use paper.

This is understandably a part of the case that gives many people particular stress. Doing math without a computer is not something that many of us are used to in our adult life. Furthermore, doing it in front of someone else compounds the stress significantly.

I can definitely say that as someone who gives a lot of case interviews, the math portion is the piece where it has the potential to go VERY wrong. I've seen far too many interviewees (all of whom were without a doubt clever and able to get the right answer) go to pieces when trying to do a calculation that is in all honesty at the same level as that given as homework to my ten year old daughter.

> *"The case is not meant to be any kind of math Olympiad. If your calculations become horribly complicated, you've probably taken a wrong turn."*

I hope you don't think I'm being rude – I completely understand the stress, and if you were to call me out of the blue and ask me to calculate, say, 7% of 140, I may well go through the same nervous reaction – sweaty palms, increased heart rate, and a sudden inability to do simple arithmetic.

"The most common mistake people make is that they get nervous and confused about the numbers. Stay calm. Use the paper effectively. Lay out a structured way of doing the calculation."

Happily, there are a number of areas we can look at regarding case math, all of which will get your skills in shape, and by the time you have finished your preparation, you should be at the point where you are actively looking forward to the math part of the case as a place where you can truly show off your skills.

A reminder of what they are looking for

First let's take a minute to remind ourselves of what they (the interviewers) are looking for, with specific regard to the math portion of the interview.

Remember the overall competencies they are looking for:

- Ability to structure a problem
- Business sense
- Judgment
- Creative thinking
- Calm and pleasant demeanor in a stressful situation

All of these can be tested by a math problem. Indeed, it would be very possible to have an interview that was solely a quantitative problem, and that interview would deliver a lot of insight into all of the above.

Remember these competencies if and when you get to the point in a case when the math rears its head. Perhaps you will get to a part of your analysis where you realize you need to crunch some numbers. Perhaps the interviewer will slide an exhibit across the table. Perhaps the interviewer will explicitly set you a math problem.

However it comes to you, you should aim to deliver the following outcomes:

Show that you can come up with a sensible and logical approach

What I so often see, and unfortunately this is the type of behavior they are explicitly trying to screen out in this kind of interview, is that as soon as a calculation presents itself, the candidate launches straight into the first step of the calculation, without considering the next steps.

> *"Don't make any kind of calculation unless you are very clear on the objective. What are you about to do and why are you doing it? What will you do with the end result?"*

Worse still, very often people will start doing calculations wherever they are on the page, often down at the bottom, and quickly end up running out of space. This sounds simple, but it's good evidence of someone who doesn't plan ahead.

> *"One piece of advice I'd give to candidates is to be thoughtful about how they want to display their own data. Think of each page of notes as a PowerPoint slide, and actually practice drawing out tables, matrices, process flows etc. There are a lot of little things you don't think about until you actually do it."*

A simple example would be that you are analyzing the profitability of a retail store. You are given some revenue numbers. You can demonstrate your natural desire to bring a structured approach by laying out some kind of table. For instance, if you have data for a number of years you could set up a table that had a top row for years, the next row showing revenues, the third row showing costs, and the final row showing profit. You may not have all of that information to hand, but it shows that you have a logical mind, and it also helps both you and the interviewer focus on what calculations you will do and what other information you might need.

For a market sizing question, you might lay out your approach first, showing the various steps you will take and the various assumptions you will make, before you launch into doing any of the calculations. Again, this shows that you like to get things organized before you jump into the work. This is exactly the sort of person they are looking for.

Use your judgment and creativity

Quantitative problems are great opportunities to show off your business judgment and your creativity. First there is the fact that you recognized that a certain piece of analysis needed to be done. For instance, in the scripted case earlier in the book, the interviewee realized that in order to analyze potential reasons for the decline in restaurant profitability it would be useful to calculate the average check size over a number of years. This was a good example of a case where the interviewer was able to supply the necessary data and the candidate simply had to do the calculation. Another common type of case involves the candidate having to make assumptions and do a quick calculation based on those assumptions. This is where your judgment and creativity can really kick in. We'll look in detail at this when we look into market sizing questions.

Show that you are happy and able to make assumptions where required

It's worth splitting this out from the bullet above, because you're not just being tested on the quality of the assumptions you make, but also on how comfortable you are making them. What do I mean by this? The interviewer is not just looking for a calculating machine who can take numbers that exist and manipulate them. The interviewer is looking for someone who will dig for data where it exists, but then continue onwards beyond the boundary of what is known. A good example of this is your willingness to make projections either in time (what will the restaurant's profitability be like in 5 years' time?) or in space (what if we opened a similar restaurant in a new market?) This is a great time to show that you are that rare individual who can combine a respect and love for data with an enthusiasm for blue-sky thinking.

Show that above all you are truly at ease doing this kind of analysis, and that indeed you are glad of the opportunity to showcase your skills

A case is a performance. One of the main differences between such an interview and a written test is that the interviewer can see how you act, and react. That means they are looking for a certain type of behavior, as well as the relevant skills. There are many nuances to the behavior that your interviewer will be looking out for, but one of the ones you don't want to demonstrate is excessive nervousness. For a job that is client facing, or that will require you to build support internally by presenting and running meetings, you need to be able to show that even in a stressful situation you can maintain a reasonably professional demeanor. Being given public math to do is an excellent test of this ability, and again is a chance for you to put your competition behind you by smiling, leaning forward, and showing that you embrace this part of the interview. If you did that, and then got the actual calculation wrong, I'd submit that you'd still be ahead of the people who got the calculation right but did so in a way that suggested that in no way should they be let loose on either clients or other important stakeholders in the company.

An overview of some useful steps to get through most math issues

For any kind of quantitative problem, there are a number of common steps that are useful to work your way through. Some are intuitive; others are not, so I'd recommend looking closely at these steps and trying to incorporate them into your own style. When it comes to your interview, you may find that some of these steps are not required, but it's best to practice them and then you can make that decision on the day.

1. DEFINE THE PROBLEM
2. SIMPLIFY
3. APPROXIMATE
4. CALCULATE
5. CHECK UNITS
6. INSIGHT

Let's work through the process with a simple case math question that you might have to solve:

"Revenues last year were $240 million, and management has given a target of 9% revenue growth for next year. How much extra revenue will need to be generated next year in order to hit management targets?"

A strong candidate will be able to answer that, using paper and pencil, in about ten seconds. A weak candidate may take more than a minute. And a strong candidate who allows themselves to get stressed may quickly turn into a weak one.

First of all, please calculate the answer and write it in the space provided (grab some paper if you're reading this on a device). You'll get a lot more out of the following discussion if you've gone through the mental effort of doing the calculation up front.

Now let's step through the process.

1. DEFINE THE QUESTION:

Whenever you set out on a math problem in a case, I'd suggest you start a new piece of paper, and write the question at the top of the page. It's very useful to have it there to refer to.

What is 9% of $240 million?

Sounds simple, but the act of defining it in such a simple way is more than half the battle, especially in a situation where you will be stressed and liable to misinterpret the question. Very often if someone gets it wrong, they will overcomplicate, and lead themselves into trouble.

For instance, we are NOT trying to solve what the total revenue will need to be next year. That would be 109% of $240 million. We should take care to notice that the question only asked us about the EXTRA revenue for next year.

2. SIMPLIFY:

Working in millions is a recipe for disaster. That's a lot of zeroes to keep track of. Since we are only doing a simple calculation here and will never be working in any other units, I'd suggest we discard the fact that this is millions of dollars, and only return to that at the end.

9% of 240

3. APPROXIMATE:

I think we can all agree that 10% of anything is easy to do. We simply move the decimal point one to the left. So 10% of 240 is 24. It's worth noting that down along with the observation that our final answer will be slightly lower than that. This is a great way of sense-checking as you go.

10% of 240 = 24.

Therefore our answer will be slightly below 24

4. CALCULATE:

Here's where it gets tricky for some. Many of us remember being taught percentages by using fractions, so might start by trying express this as 9/100 x 240/1. If that works for you, fine, but for many people it leads to trouble.

I can think of two tricks we can use, either one would get us there quickly and easily.

TRICK 1 – use the fact that 10% and 1% of anything is easy to calculate

10% of 240 is obvious as discussed above. We simply move the decimal point once place to the left. In this case it's even easier because there's a zero there so we simply remove the zero.

10% of 240 is 24.

1% of 240 is also obvious. This time we move the decimal point two places to the left.

1% of 240 is 2.4

9% is thus 10% minus 1%, so the calculation would be:

24 – 2.4 = 21.6

We could probably all do that in our heads, but if you wanted to be extra safe you could write that out longhand and do the calculation on paper, as follows. Don't feel that this is too basic a question to do on paper. It's far better to take the ten seconds and demonstrate that you value accuracy than to risk making a mistake in what is a high-stress and high-stakes situation.

TRICK 2 – calculate 1% and then multiply

This is my go-to. As discussed above you can always get 1% by simply moving the decimal point two places to the left.

1% of 240 is 2.4

Now we have a simple multiplication which I'd write out and solve on paper (do you remember how to do simple multiplication on paper? If not, look it up!). Again, don't be afraid to do it on paper. It may make you feel clumsy, but the interviewer will be happy to see that you know what you are doing, and that you show that you are serious about getting the right answer.

2.4 x 9 = 21.6

5. CHECK UNITS:

Remember we simplified this? We removed the millions and the dollars from the equation. So now it's time to put them back.

So the answer is $21.6 million.

6. WHAT'S THE INSIGHT?

You'd be amazed at the experience I usually have when I give a case with a significant calculation. People start out the case with their incredible structure. They remember that they are aiming to demonstrate their creativity, their judgment, their approach, all the while keeping their business-like demeanor.

But something happens when they get stuck into a math problem. I think it's because of the ten-plus years of muscle memory from school. They get so hung up on GETTING THE ANSWER that they forget the following:

The answer to the math problem is just a tool you will use to help you generate insight.

So they work through the number, and get to the answer, and look up at me and say:

"Twenty one point 6 million".

They do this like a dog that has just fetched a stick and has dropped it at his master's feet, and now wants either praise or the next challenge. Because that was what it was like in school. You delivered the right answer and you got the praise from the teacher, or another problem to solve.

As you approach the end of the calculation, you must ALWAYS ALWAYS ALWAYS start thinking to yourself:

"OK, I've got a hard-won answer to my math problem, but I HAVEN'T FINISHED YET. So WHAT DO I THINK ABOUT THE ANSWER? What is it telling me?"

Usually If you've done a calculation, ESPECIALLY if you were asked to do it by the interviewer, it's because the answer will enable or prove some important insight that will have a bearing on the main case question. It will probably prove or disprove one of the elements in your initial structure.

So please ensure that as you look up from the paper, you say something along the lines of;

"In order to reach the management target, the company will need to make an additional twenty one point six million dollars in revenue, which strikes me as ... " and then you deliver your insight about it being easy/difficult/impossible because of x/y/z reasons that we have already discovered in the case.

If you get an answer and you have no point of reference, there are two options, and the safest bet is to go with both.

First, use your judgment. By now you should have been discussing this issue for a while. Does $21.6 million in extra revenue seem achievable? Is there anything you can bring in from the outside world to justify your opinion? Is this an industry that is booming or is it in decline? Are we going through a recession or are customers' wallets full? How is our brand compared to competitors?

Secondly, ask yourself what else you'd need to know in order to make a sensible judgment. It may very well be that the 'other thing' is the key to cracking the case. So you may well say something like "At first glance, I don't have enough information to be able to judge whether an extra twenty one point six million dollars in revenue is achievable. So what I need to look at now is information on the market – what's the overall size of the market, who are the competitors? I'd like to understand what we know about predicted spending by the customers and what we as a company can do to either capture some of the current spend that is going to our competitors or to drive up the overall spend by customers."

So let's recap:

1. DEFINE THE PROBLEM
2. SIMPLIFY
3. APPROXIMATE
4. CALCULATE
5. CHECK UNITS
6. INSIGHT

It looks easy when we go through it like this, and in truth it is easy, so next time you are in a case interview and you realize you need to calculate something, please breathe a sigh of relief, allow a smile to light up your face, and go ahead with the calculation, fully confident that you are getting top marks for a part of the case that is leaving about half of your competition floundering.

Setting up a multi-step calculation

You're probably wondering if all case math is as easy as the example above. Unfortunately it's not, but the complicating factor is not in itself difficult.

Often you will be presented with a calculation that requires two steps. Each of the steps may be similar to the one above.

The most common way for an interviewer to construct a multi-step calculation is to have you do something in terms of either increasing or decreasing a number in the present, and then increasing or decreasing it over time.

Let's use an example:

This year our client's revenues were 45 million Euros. Our client currently has a 15% share of the market for leather shoes in France. Analysts believe that next year that market will grow by 10 million Euros. If our client adopts our strategic recommendation we believe they will be able to capture an extra 6% of that market. What would our client's predicted revenues be next year?

There are a number of things we need to do here, and this is one of those times when taking a structured and organized approach will pay huge dividends.

First of all, I'd suggest taking a moment to start a fresh sheet of paper and to write down what we know, and to write down what the question is we are trying to solve.

What will client's future revenue be (in million Euros)?

Our facts are:

Client revenue = 45M Euro

45M = 15% of market.

Future market will grow by 10M Euro.

Client could grow to extra 6% of market = 21% of future market

So - How can you lay this out on paper so that it makes it very clear what you need to do?

Here's how I would do it:

I'd draw a vertical line down the middle of my page, and write CLIENT on the top of the left column and MARKET on the right.

I'd then draw a horizontal line to give me 4 equal rectangles, and on the left hand side, for the upper row I'd right NOW, for the bottom row I'd write FUTURE.

HOLD IT! BEFORE WE TOUCH ANY NUMBERS I WANT TO CHECK IN WITH THE INTERVIEWER.

So at this point I'll say something like:

"OK, so we want to calculate future revenues for our client, making a number of assumptions. I know the starting point of 45 million Euros. From that I'm going to have to work out what the total market size was this year. Once I've got that I'll be able to calculate the future market size, and then finally from that I can calculate our client's share. As a rough check, I know that I'm going to be very roughly adding another third onto my revenues, which would take me from 45M to 60M and then there will be some extra growth on top of that, so my answer should be slightly higher than 60M Euros. Does that sound right?"

In the top left box, which is CLIENT NOW, we know that we have 45M Euro revenues.

What do we have for MARKET NOW? Well, we know that if 45M is 15% then we need to do a calculation. 45/15 = 3, which means that 1% of the market is 3, so 100% of the market is 300. So we can write 300 in the top right box. Don't forget the units. So we have 300 Million Euros.

Next I think the easiest calculation is to grow the market by 10M Euros, so for the bottom right box (MARKET FUTURE) we can write 300 + 10 = 310 M Euros. If I was doing this in a case I might draw a big arrow going from the 300M in the top box to the 310M in the bottom box.

Finally, we can address the FUTURE CLIENT box. We know that we will grow the market share by 6% to a total of 21%. So we can write 21% x 310M (the future market). That will be our answer.

21% x 310M is the same as 21 x 3.1, which I will do longhand, ending up with 65.1

As I write 65.1 and circle it I will remember to add back in units – 65.1 Million Euros.

What is the final step? The step that we must ALWAYS ALWAYS ALWAYS be thinking about?

What is the insight that this calculation can give us? In McKinsey terms, "what's the 'so what'"?

The mystery of the missing data

Often I'll give a case where the interviewee is given a piece of analysis to do like the one above, but once they lay out their calculation they realize they are missing something essential.

Every time you are given data, you should have a little voice in the back of your head reminding you that the interviewer may well be holding something back or deliberately misdirecting you.

For instance, you might get given the above question, but not be told the client's current market share. Clearly without this you can't calculate either the size of the current market or the percentage of the client's future share. As soon as you notice the missing data, you should first of all review your notes and any information you've been given to see if it is hiding somewhere, and then you should ask.

Another common hidden piece of data would be somewhere within the piece of accounting that is:

Profit = revenues − costs.

If you are ever given financial information about a company that does not contain all three of the above pieces of data, you should calculate the missing piece.

For instance, if I tell you that a company made $20 million profit on $900 million of revenues, you should be able to calculate that there were costs of 900 minus 20, ie $880 million.

Reading Charts

Another way of checking that you are comfortable using data is to give you a chart to use. Sometimes this will be in a reaction to a data request that you make ("do we have any information about customer volume in the past years?"), and at other times it may be accompanied by a question ("take a look at this chart and let me know what you think", or "here's a chart about recent profitability, what would our revenues be like next year if this trend continues?")

When the interviewer slides a piece of paper or an iPad across the table showing a chart, your initial reaction might be 'What on earth am I meant to do with this?". If that's the case, don't panic. Just smile, say "Great!" and accept the gift as if it's the best birthday present you've ever received. Then take a second to look at what you've been given and remember that it's OK to go quiet for a few seconds while you digest what's in front of you.

Once you've taken a few seconds to at least get your head around what you've been given, you might want to consider the following few points:

1. A chart can often be used to tell a variety of stories.

It's not necessary for you to pull out every piece of insight that the chart contains – the trick with this is to look for the MOST USEFUL story.

Hint. You get to decide what's most useful. Think about the question you're trying to answer. Think about some of the things you laid out on your initial structure. Think particularly about what you were discussing just before the interviewer slid the chart across the desk.

One way of decoding this is often to ask yourself what title you would give this chart if you were to present it. To think slightly outside of the box, if you were presenting this as evidence in a court case, what argument would you be proving by using this chart?

2. A chart often contains something noteworthy and surprising.

Think about it. If everything in the chart was absolutely 'business as usual' and to be expected, it's unlikely that it would have been given to you. So look for what is counterintuitive. What is surprising?

3. A chart is often good at showing comparisons.

Remember earlier on we talked about 'What's changed?' If you've been given a chart that has a time series on it, for instance revenues over a set of years, then you should be looking for some point where the line of best fit has deviated. Once you've found it, you can quantify it, and then voice the key question, for instance:

"I notice that for three years revenues were stable, and then in Year X they started to decline. I wonder what happened?"

Another useful comparison is against a competitor or against some kind of benchmark (a term consultants often use to describe a useful comparator). So if you are given data for your client AND your client's competitor, it would be useful to scan it quickly to see where the major differences are, for instance:

"I see that our client and their major competitor have similar revenues, but the competitor has lower costs. I'd love to know more about that."

4. A chart is often incomplete.

As I mentioned above, you are very often given some data in a situation where you will need to use it to calculate or infer the really useful piece of information. So for instance if you are given a time series of revenues and costs, you might find it useful to quickly calculate and note down the profit. Or if you are given costs to compare, you might want to turn each cost into a percentage, so that you can then compare with costs of another company or a benchmark. Even if it turns out that this wasn't needed, such a calculation shows that you are comfortable using data.

5. Where there's one chart, there's often another.

Don't assume that just because the interviewer only gave you one chart, that's all there is. If when you review it you realize that you still don't have all the information you need, ask if there is more information available.

Quality of Thinking

Business sense

A lot of what we've covered so far is about the way you think. Unlike a normal test, the case interview deliberately sets out to give you a situation you probably haven't thought of before and in doing so tests your ability to think, not the content of your memory.

However, there are still significant points to be gained from walking in to a case interview with a good understanding of the world you will be working in. If you are interviewing for a 'general' job like consulting, then you will need to be able to display your knowledge of (and therefore your passion for) business news and concepts. If you are interviewing for a specific industry, for instance tech or pharma, you equally have the opportunity to show your expertise and passion for that industry.

I think there are two issues worth talking about here:

1. How can you develop, or increase, your business knowledge?

2. How can you get it across in the interview?

How can you develop or increase your knowledge?

This isn't a trick question, and the answers are probably obvious to you as I lay them out, but I think it's worth taking a moment to consider, and especially to prioritize.

Let's lay out a description of the ideal candidate. You can see where you already fit, and where you might want to raise your game. I'll describe a 'generalist' candidate and you can develop your own analogue for any specific industry (the concepts will be similar).

You are well read on 'perennial' business concepts, and also on latest issues that you keep up to date with by daily reading of key business media and also weekly reading of magazines such as The Economist and Bloomberg Business Week. You have read a number of seminal business books (often to be found at airport bookstores and often quoted widely by other business articles) and can quote concepts and their originators. You can also quote specific examples of companies who have stood out in various business ventures (not just Apple).

You frequently find yourself thinking about ways to either start or improve businesses. Whenever you are stuck in traffic you think of ways to improve the flow. When you are queuing in a coffee shop you wish you could re-arrange the way the staff work. When you see an example of excellent customer service you have a good understanding of what has happened in the organization to enable this. When you hear about an organization that is doing well, you want to know more to discover how they do it, and when you hear about a company that is not doing well you believe that if you were 'given the keys' you would be able to do better.

You have chosen to study business in a formal setting, probably either an undergraduate major in business or an MBA. Through this study you have developed a well-equipped 'toolkit' of business concepts. Through your studies you have also had the chance to meet with many other people who share your passion, so much of your social conversations also revolve around business.

You have learned a lot from experience, having worked your way through some of the major business concepts through trial and error with your own ventures. Thus for most concepts you come across you can make a connection to something you have tried in your own project, which could have been a company you founded, a working practice you improved, or a non-profit or social venture that you founded or improved.

Does some or all of this describe you?

Probably you can check some of the boxes but not all.

My advice would be to start at the top, and then focus on the first one or two activities that crop up that you haven't yet done.

The easiest and most effective out of all the above is to simply increase your intake of information. If you are currently reading fiction and watching drama in your spare time, then consider putting some of those pastimes aside for a while and focusing on business media. My single biggest recommendation and one I give to all MBA students I work with is to regularly read The Economist. I don't mean skimming the headlines in the RSS feed. I mean sit down with the magazine and actually read the full articles.

If you already check the media boxes but have never tried putting anything into action yourself, consider how you could build up that experience. If you currently have a job, look around you for 'extra credit' activities that you could get involved with that would give you a sense of creating or improving a workflow or product. If you are a student, consider starting a social or community based organization, or get involved with an existing organization that could use some help. You'd be amazed how much richer your interviews will become once you can start relating concepts back to your own experiences.

How can you demonstrate your knowledge in the interview?

All of the above means nothing if you keep it secret. Put simply, every time you meet someone in a job interview, the only things they end up knowing about you are the things you tell them. This sounds so obvious but please take it seriously. If you read The Economist, or you started your own company, or you love the business style of Jack Welch, and you feel like you'd like someone to know that about you, the only way to let them know is to tell them. So tell them.

(A lot of candidates I work with keep a lot of information back because it's on their resume and 'they don't want to appear repetitive'. You MUST assume that the interviewer has not read your resume. Even if they have it in front of them, if you want to ensure they've absorbed a particular point, say it out loud and point to the resume.)

So how do you 'show off' your business knowledge?

Simple.

Fill the case with ideas to show you bring a lot of thinking and knowledge to every situation. Relate each part of the case and each point in question to something you've read or experienced whenever possible.

Often in a case you are at a point where it is up to you to provide some thoughts. It could be the opening, when you are outlining the high level concepts, it could be later on, when you are diving deeper into one of the areas for discussion. At any of these points, aim to get a variety of ideas, and where possible fix them to examples either in the case or the real world (from your knowledge or your experience).

For instance, let's go back to the restaurant case that we ran through at the start of the book. The prompt is that one location has been losing money, and you are asked to come up with a strategy to investigate and solve the problems.

Many candidates will take a minute and jot down some thoughts, then come back with something like:

Example 1.

"Well, I'd like to look at the profit of the restaurant in question. Profit is a function of revenue and costs, and revenue is a function of price times volume. Cost can be broken down into fixed cost and variable cost."

This is the absolute bare bones of what you get could away with. It's not wrong, but it's not going to be the winning answer.

A better answer would contain the same factual content, but would do a better job of showcasing the interviewee's knowledge, for instance:

Example 2.

"I've never worked in a restaurant, although obviously I've been to many in my life, and I'm always interested in the way they run. I know this is just a hypothetical case but I'd actually love to work on something like this, because I'd be really interested to get into the workings of a restaurant and see if it could be made more efficient or more profitable! So, if I think of my own experience as a customer and also imagine what's going on in the kitchen and the back office I'd break down the finances of the restaurant into revenues and costs. Those revenues come from the diners, and are going to be a function of not just how many diners you get in a given period, but also how much each one of them spends. I remember reading an article in a business magazine recently about fast casual restaurants, which I think is a big category in the US, and which I think this restaurant might fit into. The article stated that a lot of the profit came from alcoholic drinks, so I'd certainly want to look into that. Before we move on from revenues, I'd also want to look at the bigger picture. We've been in recession for a while now and I'd be really interested to see how that's affected discretionary spending. You'd think it would go down but I also read a really interesting piece in The Economist that said that when times are bad, certain types of comfort spending actually go up, and I believe fast casual dining is in this category.

If I think of costs, I'd break those down into ingredients and staff. I think ingredients would probably be fairly stable across the chain of restaurants, although that might depend on how local the purchasing is, and I've definitely observed a trend towards local ingredients, particularly at high end restaurants. In terms of staff, again the rates of pay are probably relatively constant across the group unless you've got something interesting going on locally. For instance, the town I grew up in was a vacation town, so in summer you had a lot of people around but actually many of them were wealthy and didn't want to work minimum wage in a restaurant, so the people who worked in such places often travelled in from quite a distance."

I've been perhaps a bit extreme with the two examples, but you really would be amazed at the number of people who think that example 1 is perfectly acceptable. Some people naturally default to number 2 because they're talkative and if that's the case then great. But if you find yourself in practice interviews erring towards number 1, then take a minute, and remind yourself that for each thought, assumption, or statement, you should try to add a second half of the sentence that explains why you are thinking it, and where in the real world you might point to another example. As you can see from my 'ideal' example – you don't have to be using particularly obscure or 'impressive' examples. Something from your own experience, your home town, an article you read in the popular press or on Facebook – all of these show that you are constantly thinking about business, and that in the crucial interview you are they kind of person that likes to make connections.

Judgment

In the prior paragraphs, I suggested that each time you make an assertion or raise a new issue, you should aim to follow it up with some link to the 'real world'.

Another aim, wherever possible, should be to combine that real world link with a judgment as to the relative merits of each line of thought.

What do I mean by that?

Let's think it through. At the beginning of the case you lay out a fairly exhaustive set of areas that you'd like to talk about. You do this because you want to show that this is how you work – you like to show you can bring structure to messy situations, and all of the good things we talked about in the chapter on structure.

But let me share with you a secret about the way that many situations actually play out in real life – whether in a consulting engagement or a project at a company:

Effort, energy and resources very quickly converge on the likely solution.

Let's go to the restaurant example. When we hear the initial problem, if we are being diligent we might say in the upfront section that we want to look at a range of costs including staff, utilities, rent, ingredients etc., as well as a range of factors affecting revenue.

Do you think that all of those costs are equally likely to be the problem?

If you merely list them out, and wait for guidance as to where to look first, or if you simply ask 'do we have data on costs?', then the interviewer is forced to assume that you are great at structure, but that you were born without the ability to use your own judgment.

Because if you used your judgment, you'd probably say something like:

"I'd like to look at the main costs that a restaurant incurs to see if any of them might be leading to the loss of profit in the one particular location. If I think about the types of costs, I'd think of rent, staff and ingredients costs, plus some others like utilities, back office etc. In terms of the impact of these costs, I'd imagine that rent, staff and ingredients are by far the largest – I don't think that the amount of electricity used is going to be a deciding factor of whether a restaurant succeeds or fails. And then if I think about which elements might change depending on location, I'd actually start with rent. I'd imagine wherever the restaurant was located it would pay somewhere close to minimum wage, and I'd also imagine that input ingredients cost a similar amount across the region. So let's start by diving into rent – do we have any information about comparative rents across the restaurant group?

Another way of describing this goal of adding your own judgment is that you are giving voice to the internal discussion that you should be having as you think through the case. Every time you think of something, there's another part of your brain that assesses how good an idea it is that you've just had. We get pretty good at listening to that voice internally and thus filtering our output to the rest of the world. A case interview is a time when you want that dialogue to happen audibly – it's a great way to give the interviewer exactly what they are looking for, which is a conduit into your brain to see how you think.

Creativity

Many cases are set up to push your thinking beyond the obvious. There are many ways to describe this – 'out of the box', 'blue sky', or just plain 'creative'. What all of these mean to me is that the interviewer is looking to hire someone who is not just a regurgitator of facts (now we have computers for that kind of thing), or a mindless follower of protocol (if that were the case you'd be going through a very different kind of screening process), but somebody who can take a situation, probably make some new connections based on past knowledge or experience, and then when required come up with something new.

We most often think of creativity in the arts, where the process I just described may be used to come up with a new song, a new picture, or a new story. But the exact same principals apply to business.

So make sure that during the case you give the interviewer a chance to see that you are able to think creatively and more so that you enjoy doing so.

Sometimes it is obvious when you are being asked to think 'outside of the box'. If you are given an obviously creative case then you may spend your whole half hour outside of that box. An example of this would be a business idea that at first glance sounds crazy, like putting a vending machine on an airplane, or developing a line of formal dresses for men. If you get a case like that, you can be sure that the interviewer is particularly interested to test your comfort with creative thinking.

But here's the thing – if you think about creative artists and the times that they have their most creative thoughts, you might imagine scenarios where they are relaxed, at peace with the world, when their creative juices are flowing and suddenly they get the insight. A far cry from a high pressure job interview where you are sitting rigidly upright in your new suit, trying desperately to remember your own name, let alone come up with a leap of creative genius that would make Picasso envious!

Here are a few tips that I have found work well for many candidates:

1. Always seek to go beyond the obvious

Every time you list out, either verbally or on paper, a set of factors that might be important, push yourself to add one more thing to the list that is almost definitely not as important and indeed may be wrong.

A lot of candidates censor the 'crazy' or 'wrong' ideas out, as they quite sensibly want to show that they are capable of delivering the 'correct' answer. But as we discussed when talking about judgment, this is the time to verbalize that thought process. It shows that you are not just regurgitating something from a book, but are thinking for yourself, and it also puts you in a very good position where there's a chance you might come up with something that nobody else has ever said.

2. Ask permission to be wrong

You want to show you are creative. But you also want to show that you have common sense. A good way to reconcile these conflicts and still get your 'crazy' ideas out there is to preface them with something like. "I think I've got the main points here but I want to see if there's anything more creative that might also be useful", or, "I'm sure this isn't right, but just a crazy thought..., how about...". As you can see, you can use language to set up the fact that you are now moving from what is probably the right answer to stuff that is probably wrong.

3. Use analogies

Using an analogy can be a very powerful way to think through a difficult situation. It's a great communication skill in its own right, and when you are seeking to be creative, it can be extra powerful. First of all, the interviewer will be impressed at the fact that you are doing it; secondly it will probably throw up some interesting ideas.

For instance, let's say you have been asked to think about why a hospital has seen a rise in the number of patients coming to the emergency room. After you have exhausted your thoughts, you could move on to something like... "I don't know much about hospitals, but I wonder if it's worth using an analogy of something like a supermarket. If a supermarket was experiencing a rise in shoppers, I'd think about things like... have they dropped prices for something, or do they have a product that no other stores in the area have, or has another nearby store closed down, or has something happened to traffic patterns (perhaps a new one way street or major intersection is discouraging people from visiting alternatives...).

4. Put yourself in the picture

As with analogy – this is great for extra credit, and also often throws up some interesting thoughts. The trick is literally to imagine yourself in the place that the case is about. For instance, if you have been asked to imagine ways to improve productivity on a factory floor, you might imagine yourself standing on that factory floor and looking around. What might you see and hear? You might hear a lot of loud noise which impairs your ability to concentrate. You might see a lot of clutter which gets in the way. You might see a union rep talking with union members. And so on.

Game Plan

One of the most frequent questions I hear from candidates at the beginning of their case journey is 'how should I prepare?'

If I think about the many candidates I've coached, they have on average done between 10 and 50 practice cases before they felt ready. In general they spaced that practice out across a period of two or three months, although I've also seen successful candidates cram their prep into a much shorter time. And, crucially, when I talk with candidates who were unsuccessful, they commonly reflect that they didn't do enough preparation for cases. They never say that they had practiced too much.

Many people ask the question about preparation when they have just started at Business School, at which point they may be five or six months away from the actual interview. For this situation, I'd say that it's not essential to start case practice immediately, particularly as there will be many other elements of school that will take your attention.

Some useful steps you could lay out for yourself might include:

Watch someone else do a case. Whether this is a small setting or a large public performance put on by your case club or consulting club, it is really really helpful to see an example of a case before you dive in.

Start work on structures. As described in this book in the section on structure, get into the habit of setting yourself a case question, then practice laying out the initial structure. You can do this by yourself, and it doesn't take a long time for each practice. If you did this ten or twenty times over a couple of weeks it would help immensely.

From your practice structures, you will start to notice useful and frequently used patterns. Perhaps note these down as your 'go-to' basics.

When you are ready, you will want to run through a full case. The best way to start is with someone who is an expert – perhaps a career counsellor or perhaps a more senior person at your university or company. Let them know that this is your first full run through and give them permission to take time-outs as you go through in case it is useful to give you feedback during the case. In addition, you yourself can take time-outs at any point if you want to ask questions.

After this point, you become like a pilot in training – the biggest goal is to log a lot of hours. Ideally, track down friends, colleagues and peers who are at a similar stage and get into a routine of giving and receiving practice cases. You might want to aim to do anywhere between 10 and 50 cases this way, depending on how you feel it is going.

If you can, periodically check in with an expert to get a reality check on how well you are performing.

Remember that one key part of the case is overcoming your nerves. As you practice with friends those nerves will go away and the process will become almost cozy. When you find this happening, seek out new people, people who will make you nervous.

Once you are feeling almost ready, an ideal would be to find an actual practitioner at your target company – someone who is not going to interview you on the day but who might be willing to help you prepare. Perhaps an alum of your university, or a friend of the family. These 'almost real' interviews are a great way to get company-specific pointers.

Finally, since this is a case book, I have by necessity been talking entirely about case interviews, but almost all companies will include other types of interview questions, such as 'tell me about a time when you… etc'. It is vital that you give equal preparation effort to that part of the interview. The case shows that you have some of the skills, but ultimately you will only get the job if you have the personality and experience they are looking for, so don't skimp on practicing those 'fit' stories.

Guiding principles for case prep

Here are some guiding principles I'd suggest:

- Some practice is essential.
- Most people don't practice enough, so err on the side of more rather than less.
- Aim for quality as well as quantity.
- Take time to reflect after each case.
- You can learn a lot by watching other people practice.
- You don't always have to practice a full case – drills of individual components are just as useful.
- You'll know when you're ready.

Some practice is essential

I think we can all agree on this. The case is like a dance, and if you haven't learned the steps then you can't hope to shine. Yes, it is designed to be like a real conversation, but there are definitely some parts of it that you can get better at the more you practice.

Too much practice is better than not enough

People often ask me about the perils of becoming over-prepared. In my opinion this is a concept without a lot of reality behind it. It borrows from the thinking behind athletic performance, in which presumably there is a point beyond which you are actually damaging your body if you train too much. I'd liken case prep more to something like learning how to drive a car. Is there such a thing as being over-prepared to drive a car? Clearly not, because we spend our whole lives doing it without getting noticeably worse!

I think people are scared of getting to a point where their delivery is no longer spontaneous and natural. They don't want to come across as 'wooden' and 'rehearsed'.

Here again I'd use an analogy of a stage performance. When you see a great actor on stage, and their performance is utterly natural and believable, do you think that they have achieved that through a fine balance of some, but not too much, rehearsal? I don't think so. I think a great performance is the result of a huge amount of preparation, in fact often a lifetime of preparation. A concert pianist does not do 10 or 20 hours of practice for a concert and then deliberately stop rehearsing for fear of becoming 'wooden' – they will know that the better prepared they are, the more that their own flair will be able to come across.

In fact, I'd say that the point of becoming 'wooden' and 'over-rehearsed' is a stage that you get to quite early on in your preparation. The way to get through that stage is not to stop preparing, but to continue, until you realize that you are no longer relying on memory and guidelines, but are now using your own instinct. And the more you practice, the better you'll be able to judge whether you're doing well or not.

Quality is as important as quantity
What do I mean by quality?

A lot of this is about the people you are practicing with. Very often the most available resource to you will be other people who are at a similar stage, especially if you are at a university or business school where there are many others practicing cases. There's nothing wrong with practicing with your peers like this as long as you recognize that by itself it may not be enough to get you across the finish line.

Ideally you will also be able to find people who know what they are doing. Perhaps these might be people more senior than you at school who have already been through recruiting and were successful. Perhaps this might be a career counsellor at your school who was a consultant in a former life (there are actually quite a few of us out there!). Perhaps you will pay to use a service like Evisors where you can find a large number of people standing by to give you case practice. And finally there may even be the chance to do practice interviews with members of the company you are hoping to get a job with.

Take time to reflect

Whether you have done a practice case by yourself, with a peer, or with an expert, it is always useful to make time afterwards for proper reflection.

The default process for many people is to finish the case, then to put it out of their minds as much as possible, as if it was a slightly nasty chore they've just finished.

Don't be like this. Even if (especially if) the case didn't go well, you should schedule a block of time to sit down and review your performance. Work through each of the following areas:

Structure: Now that you've done the case, could you go back and design the perfect structure?

Analysis: Are you happy with the way you laid out the logic of any calculations? Did you get the best insight from the charts? Did the case reveal any weakness in your math ability and if so, can you design or find online any practice sets to help you overcome that weakness?

Creativity: Did you nail the creative thinking part of the case? Give yourself another ten minutes to really think outside of the box. What else could you have come up with? Perhaps do some online research into the case question to see if you can find out what really happens when companies face this kind of issue.

Finally – bearing in mind that you may well come up against a similar case in a real interview, is there any kind of cheat sheet or memory aid that you could put together to help ensure that you always shine in this kind of case?

You can learn a lot by watching other people practice

If you are in a situation where there are a lot of people practicing, it is very useful to gather in small groups and run through some cases 'in public'. For instance, you could get four or five people in a room, have one person give a case, one person take it, and the others watch. Probably the people watching will get just as much out of the experience as the person taking the case. Perhaps you could then have a group discussion about the strengths and improvement areas of the person who took it (although make sure you don't dent their confidence too much!)

Most major companies also have videos on their websites of full or partial cases – these can be useful to get an idea of what that company considers as best practice, although frankly the performances are often very stilted and do not reflect the level of relaxed conversation you should aspire to.

You don't always have to practice a full case

This is a crucial point, especially if you are constrained either by time or by the availability of people to practice with.

Since we can break down a case into a number of component parts, you could also design practice drills for each component part.

Some of the most high value case practice you can do is to take a case question and to give yourself five minutes to come up with the perfect structure. Then take a break, and then come back to it and see if you could improve it. If you did one a day for a couple of months you'd end up with more than fifty perfect structures, and by that point you'd have probably developed some archetypes that you found particularly relevant and useful. Well worth the time.

Math is an easy one to nail. Since we know upfront that it will trip many people up, you can decide that you will put in the effort and be in the minority of people who walk into the interview knowing that any math question is an opportunity for you to shine. One consultant I spoke with said that before her interviews she'd spend ten minutes running through multiplication tables, just to get in the zone.

Creativity – push yourself to think of different and out of the box solutions. As you go about your daily life, look for problems that need fixing (traffic flow, design of a window display, optimal pricing of a menu, customer acquisition online etc.) and push yourself to think of something crazy that would almost definitely not work, but might then spark a whole new line of thinking. When you give a practice case, and the person you are helping has run out of ideas on a certain area, push them by asking them 'What else?' Keep asking this until they've truly exhausted all possibilities. When they have, ask them one more time by saying 'If you could wave a magic wand and literally anything could happen, what else would you do?'

You'll know when you're ready

If you get to the point where you feel happy with your case performance, where people you trust have told you that you are doing well, and where you feel happy and confident in your ability to walk into an interview and shine, then you are ready.

If you are getting consistent feedback that agrees on a certain weakness, it's probable that you need to keep working on it. The question is, are you doing anything to genuinely improve that area, or are you just continuing to practice cases without making any changes? You should always be conscious of the areas you are working on, and you should always have a plan for improving those areas, rather than just hoping they'll fix themselves with enough general practice.

Last minute prep for when the interview is tomorrow

So, the big day has almost arrived. You want to make sure you've done everything possible. What can you do at this late stage that will truly add value?

1. Review your notes briefly, but then get some rest.

If you've got cheat sheets of favorite structures, take a brief moment to go over them, but don't get obsessed. By now all of this stuff should be internalized, and you'd be better off getting some rest than cramming in one last fact or framework.

2. Ensure you've got your power clothes all set

Make sure you know what you're going to wear and that there will be no nasty surprises. For instance, make sure your favorite shirt is clean and pressed and that your tie if you will wear one is in good shape. Make sure your shoes are polished now, rather than doing it tomorrow morning which will leave your hands covered with polish!

3. Ensure you've got your supplies – paper and pens or pencils.

They'll probably supply everything you need, but best to be prepared.

4. Make sure to arrive in time to give yourself one last pep talk.

Get to the vicinity of the interview with plenty of time. Then you can go and find somewhere around the corner where you can psych yourself up. Do whatever it takes to get yourself in the zone so that when you walk into the building you are pumped up, excited, and brimming with positive energy. And remember, you're being evaluated from the minute you arrive to the minute you leave, so keep that smile plastered across your face and make sure you show everyone you meet (including the receptionist and the recruiting assistant) how excited you are.

FAQs

- Should you lead the case discussion or should you rely on the interviewer?
- How do you know when you're done?
- Do you have to do math in your head?
- How do you know when to push back or when to agree?
- What can I do to go the extra mile in the case?
- How many practice cases should I do?
- Where can I find practice cases?
- How can I find people to practice with?

Q. Should you lead the case discussion or should you rely on the interviewer?

A. This is a very common question. People often hear that they should be able to 'lead the case'. An extreme example of that would be that the interviewer might give you the question, then would sit back, arms crossed, silent, watching you talk out loud through the whole case. This is pretty rare but can sometimes happen. At the other end of the spectrum, you might get an interviewer who leads you very clearly through the discussion, reducing the case to a series of smaller questions that you simply respond to. This is actually pretty common. But how will you know in advance and how to you decide which tack to take?

The answer is to walk in to the room knowing that if required you could run through the case yourself, but to go through it with the mindset that you will be very open to what you see and hear from the interviewer. The fact is, if an interviewer wants to guide you, they will, and you'll immediately notice this. Conversely, if an interviewer is silent, you will also notice this!

If you do find yourself in a situation where you will do all or most of the talking, simply lay out your framework, and then work your way through it. At each point where you would like to ask the interviewer for information, do so. The only change to this would come if the interviewer at any time lets you know that he/she has no information or data for you. At that point, you will know that you are going to supply all of the information yourself, either in the form of assumptions, or back of the envelope calculations.

If you think through the above advice, the key here is to be flexible, and above all to respond to the interviewer. Each interviewer will have their own style, so there's no 'one size fits all' answer, but you can trust in your own ability to read the situation and to react accordingly. The only extra thing I'd add to that, is that if there is a bias either towards waiting for instruction or taking initiative then you should err towards taking the initiative.

Q. How do you know when you're done?

A. Following on from the previous question, most of the time the interviewer will give you a clear indication that the case is almost over and that you should make a recommendation. They will often say something along the lines of, "The client has just walked into the room and wants to know the recommendation, what is your answer?" Clearly in this situation you have just been told to stop the analysis and to move into your recommendation.

But sometimes (infrequently in my experience), you will not get such a prompt and it is appropriate for you to wrap up the case. So how do you know when this is true?

My advice here is to work your way through your initial structure. Remember it's your plan for coming up with an answer to the initial question. Once you've run through your plan and you do indeed have an answer, it is probably time to conclude. The trick here is that you can use language to telegraph your intention, by which I mean you can give clear warning to the interviewer that you are about to conclude. If they are actually not ready, they will stop you and let you know that there is still some analysis to complete.

For instance, you might say "Looking through my initial structure, I think we've discussed each of the areas I wanted to analyze, and we've developed a good answer to the client's question. Therefore I'd like to move to a conclusion…" Something like that is quite a mouthful, and while you're saying it the interviewer will undoubtedly have time to realize what you're about to do, so if they let you carry on, then you should move into your conclusion.

Q. Do you have to do math in your head?

A. Unless you are given clear instructions by the interviewer not to use paper, then you should always err on the side of using paper for all of your numerical calculations. (Of course, if it is a super-simple calculation like 2 + 2 then go ahead and do that in your head!). In all instances I've seen, the candidate would not be marked down for taking the time to write out a calculation. Indeed, there are many positives to this behavior – it shows that you are serious about precision, and that you take the time to get the right answer, rather than being sloppy or rushing to get an answer at the cost of being imprecise.

As discussed in the math section, the best practice is often to break the math component out into two stages – structure and then calculate. If you do this, you win a lot of points for showing that you like to plan your calculation.

Remember, you are being hired for your ability to structure a problem and then work your way through it, not because you are a calculator.

Q. How do you know when to push back and when to agree?

Sometimes in a case, your interviewer will react to something you've said by disagreeing or perhaps by suggesting a different approach or viewpoint. Candidates often ask me at this point whether they should show confidence in their own approach/thoughts, or whether they should show willingness to be flexible. Both seem like desirable qualities, so this is in my view a very sensible debate.

I've got two ways to answer this. On the whole they fit well together, but not always.

Firstly, you should always approach a case question with the mindset of enthusiastic enquiry. You are genuinely interested in getting to the right answer, and that means you set aside things like ego. Therefore, when you are challenged, the first thing to do is to act like you are pleased that someone has given a different suggestion, and then you should genuinely consider the merits of the suggestion. If after careful consideration you do not agree, then please go ahead and say so. Feel free to engage the interviewer in the spirit of open and collaborative debate. Alternatively, if you think that the interviewer's idea is better than yours, then you should thank them for their contribution. What you shouldn't do is simply ignore the interviewer's suggestion.

Secondly, bear in mind that the interviewer has a good view of the way the case is meant to go. When you start by drawing out or talking through your initial structure, it is often the case that some parts of that structure will not lead to the answer. Often the interviewer will not want you to spend a lot of time in that line of inquiry. So you will often get genuinely useful guidance from the interviewer, for instance, they might say "in this case we know it's not an issue of cost, so let's focus on the revenue side of your structure." Clearly in this instance you should follow their lead.

Q. What can I do to go the extra mile in the case?

A. Some interviews may be set up such that you could go through the structure, do the analysis, get the right answer, yet still not get full marks. How can you be sure you've always gone as far as you could? I think there are two areas where many candidates could improve:

Bring it back to the numbers

In my experience, the key is often to bring some numerical analysis back into play right at the end. Let's say for instance that we have identified that our client's restaurant is losing money because people are spending less each visit, and our main recommendation is that we develop a fixed price 'pre-theater' menu. This may be the right answer, but the extra credit answer would be then to do a quick piece of analysis. A good watch-word here is 'breakeven'. For instance, assuming the same number of customers, and assuming half of them agreed on the fixed price menu, how much would we need to charge for that to bring our revenues back up in line with the rest of the group? Or you could do it a different way, pick a price that you think is reasonable and then work out what percentage of customers would need to choose this option in order for it to return the restaurant to profitability. Either way you are demonstrating that you are somebody who is always looking for a way to bring quantitative analysis to bear.

If you suggest such analysis and start to dive into it, and the interviewer doesn't want you to spend the time on it, they'll let you know. But either way you'll get the credit for suggesting it.

One quick thought on ways NOT to look for extra credit. Don't go including a lot of new thoughts in your final conclusion. It may be that as you are delivering the recommendation you suddenly think of a new line of enquiry, but this is not the time to start mentioning that. It would ruin the effect of your crisp recommendation.

Stay positive, inquisitive and excited

I'll describe two candidates to you here. You decide which one you'd most like to hire to join you on your team:

Candidate one. They walk in visibly nervous. You welcome them and give them the case question, and at that point, they put their head down, start writing on their page, and ignore you. When you give them information that will require some calculation, they sigh audibly, and settle in to the calculation like a child being dragged to his homework. When you challenge them and suggest a new line of enquiry, they seem annoyed.

Candidate two. They walk in nervous but making an effort to be friendly. When you give them the case question their eyes light up and it is clear that they are very interested by the subject area, even if they've never thought about it before. When you give them data to analyze they eagerly dive in, even if it takes them a while to get through it. When you suggest a new line of enquiry they are genuinely enthusiastic about getting to the answer.

This is clearly an extreme, but I'm guessing you'd rather hire candidate two! So if the answer is so simple, then why is it that I see people in interviews manifesting all of the behaviors of candidate 1?

The answer is they forget the purpose of the case. They think that their behavior doesn't matter, or that if it does that it comes a distant second to the academic exercise of getting the right answer. Nothing could be further from the truth. I've heard from countless candidates who told me that they had a really enjoyable interview, really loved the case, really bonded with the interviewer, yet are sure that they missed out a key piece of analysis or know that they got something wrong. These people very often get the job.

Q. How many practice cases should I do?

A. As a general rule you should be aiming to get more than 10 cases under your belt, and ideally quite a lot more. Some people do as many as 100. As you get into your practicing, you'll eventually get to the point where you feel you have a really good understanding of the way a case is meant to be done, you'll be getting some good feedback from people you practice with, and you'll genuinely feel that if you were to walk into a real interview you'd have a good chance of displaying all of your strengths in the competencies we've discussed. If you get to that point, you're ready.

Q. Where can I find practice cases?

A. There are a number of excellent books that have many practice cases. David Ohrvall and Marc Cosentino are the authors of the most popular. Either one of those would give you plenty of practice. I think Ohrvall's is better if the person you will be practicing with is also a beginner, because it gives a lot of guidance for the person playing the interviewer. Cosentino's is better if you like to be given pre-defined things to memorize, but I think you should only use such memorized elements as thought-starters for your own customized framework for each case. Victor Cheng's book gives excellent insight into the mind of the interviewer.

If you are at a university or business school, hopefully there will be a consulting club or another type of career club where people will get together to do practice cases. If that is the situation, then the club will also probably have access to 'case books' – collections of cases that students at your school and other schools have put together over the years.

In addition, you can set yourself case questions from many walks of life. Pick up the business pages of the paper and see what stories are prominent. Ask yourself what kind of business issue was behind each story, and then get into the habit of working out which structure would have allowed you to dive into that issue.

Q. How can I find people to practice with?

A. If you are not at a university with a group of people who are also going through case practice, it can be a challenge to find people to practice with. You really want to find people who know what a case is, but who are not evaluating you. Do you have anybody in your network who is, or used to be, a consultant (but does not currently work for your target company)? Do you know anybody who went to business school? If there is nobody who can help you, there are a number of websites where you can connect with people who want to practice.

About the Author

Stephen Pidgeon is Associate Director in the Career Development Office at the Tuck School of Business at Dartmouth College, which is consistently ranked amongst the world's top Business Schools.

In his role at Tuck, Stephen helps students get internships and full time positions in all of the top consulting companies (including McKinsey & Company, Bain & Company, The Boston Consulting Group), and many other employers including Microsoft, Amazon, Google, Apple, Genentech, and Samsung.

Each year, Stephen counsels hundreds of students, helping them navigate the recruiting process, and coaching them to succeed in case interviews.

In addition, Stephen is a faculty advisor for Tuck's OnSite Consultancy program, and First Year Project, and a Senior Advisor to Resource Systems Group. In all of these roles he manages consulting projects with global clients.

Prior to working at Tuck, Stephen was an Engagement Manager at McKinsey & Company, based in the London office, during which time he served top leaders of many global organizations. He was particularly active as an interviewer, attending company presentations on campuses, mentoring candidates, and taking part in countless interviews and decision meetings.

Stephen received his MBA from the Tuck School of Business in 2007.

Stephen lives in Vermont with his wife and two daughters, and when he is not counseling students or doing consulting work he spends his time renovating his house or working in the backyard.

Printed in Poland
by Amazon Fulfillment
Poland Sp. z o.o., Wrocław

18719585R00081